George William Cox

History of the great Persian War

From the Histories of Herodotus

George William Cox

History of the great Persian War
From the Histories of Herodotus

ISBN/EAN: 9783743316676

Manufactured in Europe, USA, Canada, Australia, Japa

Cover: Foto ©ninafisch / pixelio.de

Manufactured and distributed by brebook publishing software (www.brebook.com)

George William Cox

History of the great Persian War

A YACHTING CRUISE IN THE SOUTH SEAS.

BY C. F. WOOD.

HENRY S. KING AND CO., LONDON.

1875.

PREFACE.

DURING the last eight years I have made several voyages amongst the South Sea Islands; and although so much has been written and re-written about them, I have been induced to publish these few imperfect sketches of my last cruise by the belief that any facts relating to the manners and customs of these islanders, should not be allowed to perish.

In this cruise, I was accompanied by Mr. George Smith as photographic artist, who most ably performed his part, often under the most trying circumstances.

The opportunity of taking portraits of these people in their primitive condition will soon be lost, so rapid is the advance of so-called civilization. It is a melancholy fact, that wherever an English colony is planted, there the inferior race dies out.

The policy that annexes Fiji, tolls the knell of the Polynesian race. Speculative, money-grasping Europeans will now spread themselves over the other islands of the Pacific, being well assured that land bought from the ignorant native will, in due time, be secured to them by the protection of the British flag.

Before these pioneers of civilization, the present self-satisfied, lotus-eating Polynesian, whose character is as plastic as clay, will no doubt rapidly disappear.

And while yet learned ethnologists are differing amongst themselves as to the origin of this most romantic people, it seems by no means improbable that the whole race, leaving no history and no monuments, will have passed away from the face of their Ocean.

YACHTING CRUISE IN THE SOUTH SEAS.

CHAPTER I.

EARLY in November, 1872, I left Liverpool by the Cunard line, and crossing the American continent by the Great Pacific Railway, sailed from San Francisco for New Zealand, calling at the Sandwich Islands. I reached Auckland on the first day of the new year.

The season for sailing with any degree of comfort in the tropics does not commence till April, so I took my time in looking out for a vessel that suited me. And the month of February saw me the possessor of an Auckland-built topsail schooner of ninety-two tons.

I at once set to work to make her more suitable for my purpose, by making a dark room for photography, and additional cabin accommodation for myself.

To admit carpenters into a house or vessel is simply to illustrate the fable of the snakes and the porcupine. And these men spent a month in sharpening their tools, varied by occasionally driving in a nail, or in planing a board, with the sole apparent object of making more shavings, on which to sit down and eat their dinner. At length the work was finished, and from hold, deck, and cabin

"The parting genius was with sighing sent."

The captain and crew being engaged, and all our stores on board, we moved off into the stream, and on Saturday, April 18th, sailed out of Auckland Harbour. We were not destined to get far, for when we reached the island of Motu Tapu, and were just opening out the Hauraki Gulf, a gale sprang up in our teeth from the N.E., which necessitated our running back and casting anchor under the shelter of a reef of rocks that runs out from Rangitoto Island. Presently a brig came sailing past, but she too could make nothing of the weather, and had to put back and anchor near us. Shortly afterwards the American mail steamer came out, hoarsely bellowing us a farewell with her steam whistle; but when daylight broke next morning, we found she too had had to put back, and was anchored not far from us. The gale continued all Sunday, but as it appeared to moderate on Monday, we ventured out; but towards noon it freshened again, and we ran in and anchored in Bon Accord harbour, at the back of Kawau Island, about thirty miles north of Auckland.

Here we found a whole fleet of wind-bound vessels of all sizes. Shortly after anchoring I received a message from Sir George Grey, the owner of the island, inviting me on shore, an invitation I was very glad to avail myself of. I took a long walk with him through his extensive grounds. The island, naturally most picturesque, has been much improved by the judicious planting of all sorts of pines and cypresses from every part of the world, and round the house large gardens have been laid out, well stocked with all the English fruits. In fact a young New Zealander who has never seen England, would here be able to form an idea of what an English country place is like. There must be something peculiar about this climate, for I saw growing in close proximity to gooseberries, currants, and strawberries, such tropical plants as cinnamon, ginger, coffee, and bananas. The covers round the house are abundantly stocked with pheasants and Californian quails, and occasionally a monster kangaroo would bound away on our approach. On the top of a hill that overlooks the sea, I was shown a colony of New Guinea kangaroo, remarkable from their habit of living in trees. Much of the island yet remains to be brought under cultivation, and retains the sub-tropical appearance of the ordinary New Zealand bush, but I returned on board feeling as if I had had a glimpse of my native land.

The bad weather still continued, causing a most vexatious delay, and the only resource we had was fishing. Fortunately we had excellent sport, catching more snapper and kawai than we could eat, so the crew were employed in salting them, for I knew that though we thought little of them now, they would be looked on as a great luxury in the tropics, where one has a perpetual diet of indifferent pork and worse fowl.

On Saturday, April 26th, the glass had risen and the bad weather appeared to have broken up, so we sailed out of the harbour.

The barometer, however, was delusive, and fell as fast as it had risen. Bad weather still impeded our progress, and when we reached the neighbourhood of Sunday Island, we met with a very tempestuous sea. Heavy and irregular seas are the rule in the neighbourhood of this group, and I have always experienced them here myself.

Masters of vessels will tell you this arises from an uneven bottom. This may be the case, for Sunday Island itself is volcanic, and only a few years ago suffered such a shock as to alter its whole appearance. An enterprising Yankee who had taken up his quarters here, and made a living by supplying whalers with fresh provisions, was at that time obliged to leave, and I do not know that he has ever returned.

On Thursday, May 8th, in gloomy and boisterous weather, we saw high land looming through the mist. This proved to be Mount Washington, that forms the western end of Kendavu, the southernmost large island of the Fiji group. Leaving this to the eastward we sailed on north, and next day sighted the low and rugged island of Biva, while at a greater distance we could just distinguish the lofty and picturesque outline of Waia, both belonging to the Fiji group. The weather now was intensely hot and fine, and that feeling of drowsiness and languor came over me, which I have always experienced on first reaching the tropics. Reading becomes a delusion and a snare, and to take up a book means to be asleep in a few minutes. On Sunday, May 11th, we sighted Rotumah. This was the first island I intended visiting, my object here being to ship some of the natives, to strengthen my present crew. No one ought to attempt a voyage through the South Sea Islands without carrying an extra crew of this kind. For in the first place there are so many islands where there is no anchorage or perhaps a very precarious one, that it is better to keep the vessel standing off and on, worked by the white crew, while those who wish to visit the island go away in the boat manned by the South Sea Islanders. A coloured crew, too, are better able to row about all day in the hot sun; they are cheery, light-hearted companions, and are always ready, and enjoy the fun of diving into the water after any shell or piece of coral that one may fancy whilst rowing over the reefs.

In addition to this, when amongst doubtful or treacherous natives, they are quicker than white men in detecting any signs of roguery, or more serious treachery, and are not so easily thrown off their guard. We got up to the land in the afternoon, and rounding the north-east end of the island, ran close past a small islet called Hama, and dropped anchor in fourteen fathoms, the small islet bearing east by north, about half a mile distant—the main land about a mile and a-half.

This is the best anchorage at Rotumah, but though well protected from the prevailing south-east trade-winds it is by no means a snug one, for should the wind fly round to the north, it is better to get up the anchor and stand out to sea at once, rather than wait till a northerly swell comes rolling in, with the dirty, unsettled weather that usually accompanies a wind from that quarter. As soon as the anchor was down, a whale boat, manned by natives, came off from the shore, and amongst the crew I recognized several old friends who were delighted to see me, and soon went off again to acquaint the people on shore of my arrival.

Rotumah is about thirteen miles long and four or five broad. From the sea it appears to be clothed with cocoa-nuts to the very summit of the hills. These are of moderate height, none, I should say, exceeding 1,000 feet. The soil, though extremely fertile, will never be fitted for clearing and planting by Europeans on any large scale, for the greater part of the island is covered with scoriæ, which could only be cleared off at great expense. All the available land near the coast is occupied by native plantations, whilst the interior of the island is surrounded by stone walls, and is entirely given up to pigs.

These range the bush in a half-wild state, though every native professes to know his own pigs, which is scarcely credible. Occasionally, natives go up into the pigs' country, and chop up cocoa-nuts for them, summoning them to the feast by blowing on a conch shell or beating with a club against a hollow tree. I have gone up with them to witness this, but as often as not, no pigs answered to the summons.

Though the climate of Rotumah is decidedly a wet one, rain falling almost every day, there is not a single stream on the island, and the natives are entirely dependent for their water supply on a number of small wells varying from fifteen to twenty feet in depth.

The coral reef, though in some places extending two miles from the land, has no depth of water inside it, and is in many places quite dry at low water. Thus, though the reef affords no shelter to vessels visiting the island, it forms an excellent fishing-ground for the natives. Every retiring tide leaves an abundance of fish in the rocky pools about the reefs. I have spent some very pleasant hours in this way, going out in my boat, with a native crew, who, on arriving at one of these pools would dive down, while I, from the surface, could watch them searching every hole and cranny of the coral rock. They seldom return to the surface without some bright-coloured fish, this they would throw into the boat; one long breath fortifies them for a second descent; and as soon as the splash of their dive had subsided, I could see their dark brown forms again, far below me, as they searched for more fish.

On Monday morning, Mr. Smith went on shore

with all the pomp and circumstance of photography, and caused no small excitement. The men carrying tents, cameras, etc., formed quite a procession, and I watched them from the vessel winding away amongst the cocoa-nut groves that fringed the shore. The party did not return till evening, whilst I spent a busy day on board, trading with the natives for provisions, which can be got here in any quantity. Finding I wanted to ship a few hands, any number of young natives volunteered to go. But I selected four, who came on board with permission from their chief to go away with me. At night the wind shifted round to the north and we had to get up the anchor and go out to sea. We passed a wild and stormy night, torrents of rain falling, with much thunder and lightning, but, with the morning, the wind went back to its old quarter, and we ran in and anchored again.

The natives crowded on board, and the vessel was perfectly surrounded by boats and canoes, bringing island produce. The noise they made was deafening, and, considering what a miserable night we had had, was almost more than I could endure.

On the 16th we went up in the boat to Noatau, a

town about four miles to the south, taking the photographic apparatus, for I was particularly anxious to get some portraits of the natives.

We did not, however, meet with much success, for, strange to say, these people, so civilized and so keen and sensible in any matter of trading, could not be persuaded to look upon being photographed in anything but a ludicrous light. For did one of them after much persuasion consent to sit, then a crowd would gather round, especially the women, and by tittering and laughing and making remarks, make the intending subject such an object of ridicule that he would fairly take to his heels. So that when poor Mr. Smith, who had been perspiring in the tent preparing a plate, reappeared upon the scene, he would be greeted with a silly shout of laughter, and have to begin his solicitations again for a fresh subject. Some of the chiefs at last submitted to be taken, but even then the people's natural respect for their rulers scarcely prevented them from cracking jokes at their expense. I found it very difficult to keep my temper; in fact, some people might say I did not succeed; and towards evening I returned to the vessel thoroughly fagged out.

This, our first experience of the camera amongst the natives of the South Seas, was not very encouraging.

On Monday, the 19th, we got up the anchor and ran down seven miles further to the westward, anchoring again in what is known as Lee Harbour, in fifteen fathoms. This anchorage is open to all the objections of the last, with an additional one of not allowing a vessel so much room to get under way. Off this end of Rotumah lie several small islands, only one of which, a lofty precipitous mountain, is inhabited. One of the smaller islets is very remarkable, having been by some convulsion of nature split through the centre from top to bottom; through this crack it is said that a boat can just pass in fine weather. Near the top of the crack a large mass of rock has been firmly wedged, and there hangs like the falling keystone of an arch.

On Wednesday, 21st, I accompanied the photographic party on shore, and wherever we saw a nice view, the tents were pitched, the camera fixed, the picture taken; then the whole camp moved on again till we came to anything else worth taking. In this way we went right round the bay. Near the head of the bay is a most magnificent grove of trees, of enormous size; in foliage they somewhat resemble the india-rubber tree, whilst their giant stems are gnarled like ancient olive trees. To come from the glare of the white coral beach into the shade of this grove is like plunging into a cold bath. A little further on, the island is only a hundred yards wide, and consists but of a strip of sand. The sea appears at some time to have flowed over this, and the idea is confirmed by the fact that the tribe on the western side are called the " Itu Motu " —the " Cut-off" tribe.

On the top of this sandy ridge the chief of this district has built his house. He had come to meet me on the other side of the bay, and was very anxious to have his picture taken. Delighted at finding his request was not refused, he went into his house and proceeded to array himself to the best advantage. The day was one of the hottest I ever experienced, not a breath of wind was stirring, and the rays of the sun beat down most unmercifully. Yet in spite of this, our friend put on a warm flannel shirt of some blazing red tartan, wrapped a heavy woollen shawl of a somewhat similar pattern round his loins, on the top of this put an old Russian naval officer's coat, buckled an ancient military sword round his waist, put an Inverness cape on the top of this coat, covered his head with a wide-awake hat, and grasping a telescope in one hand and an old Tower musket in the other, went forth to be photographed.

There was a murmur of approbation from his admiring retainers, as he stalked past them with all the airs of a peacock. Unfortunately for him the bath had got so hot, that the first two attempts to get a picture were unsuccessful. All this time our miserable subject was being almost stewed alive, and kept on saying, "O do be quick! I am so hot! my head is aching so." But I must do him the justice to say that he endured it all, and did not attempt to strip till the picture had been taken. He then retired to his house, where I shortly afterwards found him, in the costume of our first parents, drinking cocoa-nuts and fanning himself.

While we were anchored at the north-east end of the island, the chief of Noatau made a proposition to me, and to explain it I must begin, as he did, with history. It appears that many years ago, before the Polynesians had become demoralized and enfeebled by contact with the white man, they were in the habit of venturing on long voyages in their canoes, and there was more intercourse between the different islands than we give them credit for at this day. In Rotumah one sees at several places large double canoes, similar to those of Fiji and Tonga, lying in their sheds on the beach. The people assure me that no one now alive, or their fathers before them, have ever seen those canoes in the water. Were they to launch them, they would not know how to manage them, nor could they make the mat sails suitable for them, so completely have they lost all their former knowledge of navigation.

Many years ago, from the small volcanic island of Niuafu, some 450 miles distant, there came to Rotumah a fleet of war canoes headed by a chief named Maraff. They effected a landing, and, overcoming the natives, settled on the island. In course of time Maraff died, and the whole party appear to have returned. The Niuafu title of Maraff was then adopted by a Rotumah chief, and to the present time the chief of the Noatau tribe always succeeds to that title.

A year or two ago, the present chief of Niuafu, descendant of the old invader, sent his Rotuman namesake an invitation to come and see him, saying that he was anxious to look him in the face; and the ambassador appears to have given the Rotuman chief to understand, that many of the people of Niuafu were anxious to leave their island and become settlers in Rotumah. For the people were terrified at the frequent volcanic outbreaks; while the exactions of King George of Tonga, whose subjects they are, and the oppressions of the mission society, were also hinted at.

Maraff's proposition to me was that I should carry an ambassador for him to Niuafu, to say that as many of the people as liked to come would find with him a welcome and a home.

As I intended visiting Niuafu, I consented to carry his messenger, but told him I could not bring any of the people, for I was forbidden by the laws of my country from carrying natives without a special license.

At Rotumah I found any number of people

anxious to go away with me, and I found out afterwards as I went from island to island, that the natives would like to turn one into an omnibus, to pick up and set down passengers all over the Pacific. As it is, I have a curious collection: first the ambassador for Niuafu; then a native of Wallis Island who has nearly lost his eyesight, and is anxious to return home; then a lame little boy suffering from a painful disease in his feet, whom I have undertaken to cure and bring back again; and finally two sons of chiefs, boys of about fourteen, who are being sent by their fathers under my charge, to see the world. Their parents parted with them with much grief, begging me to see that they were good, did not do any work, and did not go to the forward part of the vessel and speak to the sailors. Large presents of pigs, fowls, and yams were sent off with them. Of course the young rascals, like fine manly boys, as soon as ever they got over sea-sickness, were for ever pulling at ropes, climbing the rigging, or sitting chatting with the sailors, and I felt convinced that it would be the worst thing possible for them to prevent it.

CHAPTER II.

DURING my stay I managed to procure, with a good deal of difficulty, some of the stone and shell implements in use by the natives before the introduction of iron. They consist of stone adzes and tomahawks, and also round balls made from the large clam shell (tridacna); these latter, formerly weapons of war, may now be occasionally met with in their houses, used for pounding food. It is difficult, among a people so civilized as the Rotumans, to gather either facts or objects of interest to an ethnologist. They state that they came originally from Samoa, which lies further to the east, and the history of the arrival of the first man and woman is mingled with the wildest legends of giants and witches. Several of the constellations are called in to play a part, notably the Pleiades and Orion. Through all their long and tedious stories runs a strain of cannibalism, though when taxed with it they deny that they were ever cannibals. The same charge might be brought against us, with our stories of Jack and the beanstalk and numerous other tales of ogres. An old man, however, admitted to me that places are still pointed out where solitary individuals practised cannibalism, to the terror of the community. One of such places was shown me—a cave on the seashore.

On my asking why the people did not combine and destroy these individuals, he said that in those days there were very few people in Rotumah.

If we look for any foundation of truth to this story, I should conjecture that these individuals were remnants of a former race.

The present race think there was a race of men before them. For I procured from them three distinct kinds of adzes: first, some polished and well finished; secondly, some coarsely made of rough stone, and similar ones of tridacna. The two latter, they say, are of their own manufacture, for either hollowing out canoes or as implements of war, "but no one can tell who made the others." Formerly they were looked on as charms. Bury them in the ground, and on going next day you would find them moved some few feet from the spot they had been placed in. I never knew natives speak more decidedly on any point than on this, namely, that they had nothing to do with these polished stone adzes; and from the fact of their being looked on as charmed I should be inclined to believe them.

The island was and is at the present time governed by six independent chiefs of six independent tribes, and in addition to these there were the two national offices of Mooa and Sou.

It is difficult to make out the exact object of these offices, but they were in every way connected with heathenism, and with the introduction of Christianity have disappeared.

The Mooa was the more important of the two, but both Mooa and Sou only held office for twelve months. The Mooa is described as being like the woman, while the Sou was like the man. But they in no way represented the Mahoos of Tahiti mentioned by Wilson and Turnbull. They were both married, and very rarely lived in the same tribe.

It was necessary that the Mooa should be a young chief of very high blood, and his election was by capture; it followed as a consequence therefore that he resided in the most powerful tribe.

When the term of office of the Mooa had nearly expired, it became necessary to look out for a successor.

The men of the most influential tribe would therefore fix on some chief of high blood of any tribe, and arming themselves, would proceed to his house and carry him off by force, when often much resistance would be offered. But once installed in the Mooa's house, no attempt at recapture would be made.

His duty now consisted in being fed night and day, in fact, systematically fattened.

Three times every night he was roused to eat, and pigs were killed every day for him, the chiefs and old men eating with him: such waste and extravagance, indeed, was practised, that the tribe in which the Mooa resided was generally short of provisions. It was for this reason, as much as any other, that the Sou, who was attended in the same way, rarely occupied a house in the same tribe as the Mooa, the expense being too great for one tribe to bear.

The Sou always resided in the second most

powerful tribe, his mode of election being similar to that of the Mooa.

Every six months there would be a grand gathering of the people at the Mooa's and Sou's house, when the priests blew on large conch shells, and called out the names of the various fruits and vegetables of the island, in order to secure good crops. Rioting and feasting were then the order of the day.

The Mooas were always buried at one spot, situated near the village of Noatau, on the south-east side of the island. They were all placed in separate graves. I have visited the place, and round about the graves scattered in the bush one still sees the old devil stones, as they are now called, but really known as "Toopoa," on which they practised some heathenish rites, but never, as they say, human sacrifices.

The Sous, on the contrary, were from time immemorial buried in one sepulchral vault. This is situated in the town of Lopta, on the north-east side of the island. With each Sou would be buried one small stone adze. When any Sou died, all the other remains of Sous were taken out, and re-rolled in fine new mats; the new corpse, rolled also in fine mats, was placed at the bottom, the others all above him, in every case recumbent.

It is difficult, as I have said before, to see the exact object of these two offices. And yet we need not look far from home to see something similar. The other day, while standing in the Temple Gardens watching the Lord Mayor's procession, a native of Rotumah, whom I had with me, astonished at the magnificence of the Lord Mayor's carriage, asked if he was a king. It puzzled me to explain his exact position, but I felt I could not define it better than by calling him the London Sou.

The Rotumans have always paid great respect to their dead. Even to this day they will spend a great deal of money in getting a gravestone from Sydney to place over some relative's tomb. On the decease of any one, immediately after the burial, much feasting and destruction of the dead man's live stock takes place; what cannot be consumed at the feast is portioned out to the guests to be carried home.

The very ancient tombs are made of enormous blocks of stone, and it is difficult to believe that a people so lazy and apathetic at the present day should ever have had the energy to move these heavy masses.

These ancient tombs resemble dolmens. Four large unhewn stones form the sides, on which one large flat one is laid for the covering. I measured one top stone, which was over ten feet square and three feet thick. But I saw much larger which I could not measure, owing to their being covered by drifting sand.

At the present time, with the exception of half a dozen houses in a valley in the interior of the island, only the coast-line is inhabited; ten or twenty years ago there were several large towns in the interior, and before that, they say the whole island was densely populated. There is good reason to believe this, for, go where you will in the interior, you come upon very large burial grounds in the dense forest, indeed the very summits of the highest hills are in nearly every case graveyards.

In Mariner's "Tonga Islands" an account is given of the voyages of Cou Moala, a Tongan chief, and of his visit to Rotumah. His name, I found, is not forgotten by them, and wonderful tales are told of his surpassing strength and activity, but on enquiry I could learn nothing of the marvellous gigantic bones that Cou Moala said he saw here.

So I fancy they were the creation of Cou Moala's brain: your travelled South Sea Islander is always a liar—even if he were not, he would always get the credit of being one. I have mentioned above, that formerly the Rotumans were possessed of large canoes; an old chief told me that many of these canoes used to sail away loaded with men and were never more heard of.

In those days a young chief, fired with a desire to see the world, would fit out his canoe, and call upon his followers to attend him, who dared not refuse; there was always great weeping and wailing at their departure, and they sailed away often never to return.

We know that some canoes from Rotumah arrived on the northern coasts of Vanua Levu in Fiji, for their half-breed descendants may be seen to this day. There appears to have been a regular system of going to the Tongan Islands to get the Cypræa ovula, a white shell used to decorate the chiefs' canoes and houses, which is not found at Rotumah. They did not buy these from the natives of Tonga, but they themselves fished for them on outlying reefs.

On one occasion a party were returning from a successful expedition after these shells, when the chief in command died. So they made a raft, and wrapping the body in fine mats, and ornamenting it with white shells, placed it on the raft and sailed on. Next morning what was their horror to see the raft in front of them. They sailed past it again, and next morning the ghostly raft appeared again ahead of them. In terror the leader of the party seized an axe, chopped off his little finger and threw it into the sea; from that time they saw no more of the raft, and arrived safely at Rotumah.

Under the influence of Christianity the people have changed much. They used to wear long hair, which in war time they tied in a knot on their head; it was an act of discourtesy, not to say an evidence of hostile intentions, for one man to approach another with his hair so tied up. They were also tattoed similarly to the Samoans round the loins and thighs, and had the nasty habit of smearing themselves with turmeric, turning their rich brown skins to a bilious yellow.

All is changed now. With Christianity comes a cropped head for both sexes, no red paint on the cheeks, no flowers ever to be worn in the hair, the heart is never gladdened by the sound of song, and all dancing of every description strictly forbidden, the young men are forbidden the almost national sport of wrestling, and all kinds of manly games. Not unnaturally therefore the first object of every lad is to run away to sea, often intending never to return. He cares not for his name received in Christian baptism, whether Ebenezer or Zerubbabel. In his heart he looks upon the name the sailors give him as his real one, whether Tom, Dick, or Harry, and this will cling to him through life. Were it not for the careful watch kept by the chiefs over vessels visiting the island, the young people would leave the island *en masse*, and Rotumah in a few years be depopulated.

Such is the result of attempting to plant Wesleyanism in the sunny climes of the South Seas—a peculiar phase of Christianity that has been bred and nurtured in the foggy, smoky, gloom-compelling climate of the north.

Geologically, Rotumah is very interesting. The currents round the island are very strong, and the sea is rapidly encroaching on the south-east. The natives with characteristic shrewdness selected this spot as the piece of ground to be given to the mission, but finding it was disappearing so rapidly the Wesleyans have procured a more durable site. I have no doubt that at one time the island extended out to the reef which is now nearly two miles from the mainland, for between the island and the reef are several small islets founded on solid rock, with perfectly bare abrupt sides, their summits crowned with cocoa-nut palms and low bushes. One islet lies on the reef itself.

On this side of the island, too, is a high sandy beach, but after crossing this the land falls below or even with the sea-level, so that were this sandy barrier once passed by the sea, a lagoon would be formed, in which the various hills would be left standing as islands, and would in course of time from the action of the currents take the same precipitous form as the outlying islets.

The Rotumans are very fond of listening to stories resembling our fairy tales. And it is a pretty sight to see a group of bright-eyed little brown bodies gathered round some one who is "telling them a story."

Here is a specimen story, as it was told to me by a chief's wife, who on my expressing a wish to hear some of their stories, was sent for as being the best story-teller in the tribe. I wrote it down at the time as she narrated it :—

"This is the story of two sisters: their names were Bigmouth and Smallmouth. One day they set a snare, and after waiting some time, went to look if there was anything caught. They found in it a swamp hen, and carried it home and cooked it. When it was sufficiently baked, Bigmouth said to her sister, 'If I can swallow it all at one mouthful you shan't have any, but all that I can't swallow at one mouthful shall be your share.' Then Bigmouth opened her enormous jaws and swallowed the bird whole. At this poor Littlemouth began to cry, for she was very hungry. But Bigmouth said, 'Don't cry; we will very soon catch another.'

"So they went out again with another snare,

which they set, and after a little time went to look if anything was caught. And in it this time they found a woman and a baby.

"When they saw her they were in great spirits. But the woman cried and begged them not to eat her, saying that she was very clever at fishing, and if they would take her home and spare her life, she would fish for them every day and get them abundance of food. To this they consented, and took the woman and child home. When they reached the house the woman said, 'Take care of my child, and I will go out fishing for you at once.' The sisters promised to take good care of the child, and the woman went out, wading away in the shallow water towards the reef. Now, no sooner was the woman out of the way, than Bigmouth pulled off one of the child's legs and began to eat it; and by the time the woman had got out to the fishing-ground, Littlemouth had pulled off the other leg and eaten it. And a strong smell was wafted across the water to the woman, so unsavoury that she could not fish. Then Bigmouth, going down to the beach, sang loud across the water, 'We will stone the swamp hen and hang the child.' And the woman sang back again, 'Feed it well; feed it well; feed it on pap that it may not choke!'

"Then Bigmouth and Littlemouth each tore off an arm and ate it, and then proceeded to tear the rest of the child's body in pieces, taking care to catch the blood in a cocoanut shell. And again a strange and sickening smell was wafted across the water to the woman as she fished, and she sang again as before, 'Feed it well; feed it well; feed it on pap that it may not choke.'

"Still the sisters continued devouring the child, till all was gone but the head. This they took, and first shaved the hair in diamond pattern, then painted it all over, and placed it near the door. They took a large piece of tappa, which they rolled up to resemble the child's body, so that it appeared as if the child were sleeping. And then sat down and awaited the mother's return.

"She presently came back, put down her basket of fish outside the door, and asked for a cocoa-nut shell of water to wash with. The sisters handed her the shell of blood. But the mother said, 'What a strange smell of blood!' And they said, 'This is one of the shells we have used to mix our paint in, and that makes the smell.'

"'Well,' said the mother, 'it certainly smells like blood to me.' However, she took it and washed herself in it, and then brought in her basket of fish. She asked for a clean dry mat to put on, for her own was wet with fishing. But the sisters said, 'Your child Konootofia is lying on the only one we have.' Not willing to disturb the child, she asked for a piece of tappa. But they answered her that the only piece of tappa they had was covering the child. However, they went and fetched some leaves of the dracæna that she might make a girdle for herself, but the woman said, 'You have not brought enough.' So they went out to fetch some more; and on the way they saw a young tree, and they stopped to enchant it, that it might grow up to the sky, and then they brought in some more leaves of the dracæna. Still the woman said it was not enough. So they went again and again; each time singing to the tree to grow quick, while the woman made her dress. Then they ran to the tree, and climbed up a long way, and there sat and sang, 'Look at your child; it is eaten!' The mother hearing this, ran to her child, and lifting up the tappa, saw that there was nothing left of it but the head. Then in a fury she ran to the foot of the tree, and tried to climb up after the sisters, but the one that had gone up last had stripped off all the bark, and the stem was now so slippery that the mother could not climb. After several vain attempts, she sat down at the foot of the tree in despair, and cried for some time. Then she went into the house, and taking her child's head in her lap, she wept over it, saying, 'Oh, what a foolish woman was I to go out fishing and leave my child! Had I taken proper care of it this would never have happened.' Then she came out of the house and sat down at the foot of the enchanted tree, and there she pined away and died.

"But Bigmouth and Littlemouth still kept climbing up, and they got so high and went so far that they came to another world. And there they saw two people grown together and quite blind. These two had each ten yams cooking on the fire, and they were also busy making a mat. Then Bigmouth and Littlemouth, careful not to make the slightest noise, crept up and each took one yam off the fire. And presently the two people turning round to the fire to ascertain if their yams were cooked, found that two were gone. And the one said to the other, 'I have lost a yam;' and the other answered, 'So have I.' However, they said no more, but went on making their mat. Then Bigmouth and Littlemouth ate all the yams but two. And when the blind people discovered their loss, each accused the other of stealing, and they began to quarrel; but their bad temper soon passed off, and they began to dance, wondering who had stolen their yams. Their dance was so good that Bigmouth and Littlemouth burst out laughing. Then the blind people knew that strangers were present, and at once put them down as the thieves who had stolen their yams, and they were very angry. But Bigmouth and Littlemouth said to them, 'Do not be angry with us, for we can do you a great service. We will give you sight; and although you are fast grown together yet we can separate you.' Then they got some herbs and some cocoa-nut oil, and they also picked up some small stinging ants. They anointed their bodies with the oil and herbs, and they came asunder. The small ants they placed on their eyes, and the ants stung them, and their eyes were opened. And then they all played at 'hide and seek.'"

This story was pronounced so excellent, that the old lady, our Polynesian Scheherazade, after a few draws at an old clay pipe, and a pull at a green cocoa-nut, commenced again as follows:—

"This is the story of a woman. A long time ago there lived a woman quite alone, but at last growing weary of her solitude, and wanting some amusement, she went to another island and walked about and amused herself. The king of that island happening to meet her, fell violently in love with her, for she was very beautiful, and after a short courtship he took her to be his wife, and in due course of time two children were born, the first a boy, to whom was given the name Ephongmal, the second a girl, who was called Sheun.

"The king's brother, whose name was Tinro, took care of the girl.

"But in course of time the king's subjects grew jealous of the queen, and brought evil reports of her to the king, telling him that she was a witch, and that he ought to have nothing to do with her. The king was at last persuaded by these reports, and sent for his son, with the intention of eating him. And the king's brother Tinro was the only one that objected.

"The mother was of course much distressed at the determination of the king to eat her son. But she comforted her boy, assuring him that it was far better to be eaten by his own father than by any one else.

"A day was appointed for the feast to come off, and the people built small huts in the town, where all might sit and see the operation. But the king refused to sit in one of these huts, preferring to eat his son in the open air. Then when the people had collected, they laid green cocoa-nut leaves on the ground, on which to cut up the boy, but he begged to be cut up on a mat and not on a green leaf. And all the time Sheun, his sister, stood by weeping and begging that she might share his fate. But her brother said, 'No; I alone will die.'

"Then they cut him in pieces and placed the heart before the king, and Sheun stood by beating off the flies with a fan. Then the mother said to her daughter, 'When I give you the signal, throw the heart at the king and run to me.' All this time the mother had been busy, she had filled an old canoe with water and had also baked some food. At the given signal the daughter threw the heart at the king and ran to her mother. The mother took up the heart and put it into the canoe full of water, and as she put it in she said to it, 'When I turn round, you turn round.' And as she spoke she turned round, and the heart turned also, and became covered with flesh. She addressed it again in the same words, and as she turned round so the heart turned, until it became a whole body and finally sat up in the canoe.

"Then the mother made her son eat the food she had baked, and they went away.

"They came to the mother's original home, and there they built a large canoe, and sailed to another land, where they were met by a very fine-looking man and woman who begged them to stop there. But Ephongmal declined, fearing that they were cannibals. They assured him they were not cannibals, and persuaded him to stop.

"The result of this was that Ephongmal married the woman, and in course of time a son was born.

"Now the woman was really all the time a cannibal, and having abstained from human flesh for some time, she felt an indescribable longing for it, and begged her brother to procure some for her. He at first refused, saying no good would come of it; but she begged so persistently, that he took her child and cooked it, and placed it before her to eat. But she, fearing her husband's wrath if he should discover that his child had been cooked, wanted to conceal the body; but her brother said, 'No; you asked for it, and it shall be known that you have got it.'

"Soon after Ephongmal came in, and was seized with the greatest distress on account of his child's death, and would not allow it to be eaten. And going down to the beach, he launched his canoe and returned home to his own island; but by the time he had got there he found that the woman had managed to reach it also by swimming. He refused to forgive her, and would not let her enter his house, and next day took her back to her own island, and returned home. Still the woman persisted in swimming back to him again; and at last, after repeated efforts to get rid of her, and finding that she would keep on swimming back to him, he took her out to sea, a long way from land, and threw her overboard, and there they say she is still to be seen."

I think my old friend would have gone on telling me stories till next morning, but I stopped her, and asked her to come another night, and so it came about that I used to have whole evenings of story-telling; but I found it rather hard work writing them down as they fell from her lips.

These are not stories invented by the teller, but the old stock stories of the island, corresponding to our Cinderella or Jack the giant-killer, or Jack and the beanstalk.

CHAPTER III.

ON May the 29th, at daylight, we sighted the lofty island of Futuna, but the wind was very light, and not until next morning could we enter the harbour of Singavi. Very few of the natives came off to us, and those who did seemed not to care about selling any provisions or trading in any way.

High up on a cliff on the east side of this little bay we could see a number of natives at work. We were informed that they were quarrying stone for their new church, which is being built under the direction of a French priest.

Every now and then, mingled with the shouts of the quarriers, could be heard the crash of some large mass of stone as it tore its way down through the tropical jungle to the beach below.

In the evening I took a stroll on shore, and was

not much comforted by the fact that nearly all the houses were built, or partly built, of wrecks of vessels, which does not speak well for the security of the harbour.

The natives are taller and darker than the Rotumans, and their hair has a tendency to become frizzly. They have a custom of flattening the backs of their heads, considering that this improves their personal appearance; this is done by placing a heavy roll of tappa on the sleeping baby's head.

Marsden mentions that this was a custom with the Sumatrans; it was also noticed by Captain Cook at Ulietea.

The Futuna people have embraced Roman Catholicism, and are certainly the most uninteresting race I ever met with. All life and native humour has left them, and they appear to have handed themselves over body and soul to the French priest, who may now be said to be king of the island; the two native kings possessing little but the empty title.

Perhaps phrenologists would be able to pronounce an opinion as to whether the flattening of their skulls has in any way influenced their character.

Early on the morning after our arrival I was

visited by a number of victims to the Fiji "labour traffic;" they were natives of Tamana, one of the Kingsmill group. Fortunately I had with me a boy from that part of the Pacific, who had been with me to England, and spoke English well, so that I was enabled to understand all they said to me.

It appears that for some years an emigration has been going on from the crowded and somewhat unproductive island of Tamana to the more fertile and thinly populated island of "Nui," one of Ellice's group.

It so happened that a Fiji vessel, in search of "labour" for Fiji plantations, called at Tamana, when a number of the natives, thirty-five in all, men, women, and children, requested to be taken as passengers to Nui. The captain consented, and they paid for their passage in pigs, fowls, mats, &c. It appears, however, to have been the captain's intention to run them to Fiji and sell them as "labour;" and the natives were much alarmed when they found the vessel had passed their intended destination.

On the passage, however, the vessel encountered very bad weather, and was obliged to put into Futuna, when the Kingsmill natives, finding that they were going to be taken to Fiji and sold there, jumped overboard in the night, even mothers holding their babies, and swam on shore. These natives, I may mention, had all embraced Christianity under that most excellent society, the London Missionary Society. They now begged me to take them away to Nui if possible, but anywhere except Fiji, that country having acquired such an evil reputation. The Futuna natives also joined in begging me to take them away, stating that they consumed so much of their provisions, for they found that the strangers, though very clever at fishing, were utterly incapable of helping them in their yam plantations, &c.

I was sorry to be obliged to refuse this, for owing to the stringent orders given to our men-of-war to seize all vessels carrying natives without a special license, I should have laid myself open to seizure by the first enterprizing young naval officer who came across me. I explained this to the natives, but promised to report their condition to the first man-of-war I met, and also to the London Missionary Society at Samoa.

I may here add that on my arrival in Fiji I reported this to the captain of H. M. S. "Dido," and as the guilty vessel arrived shortly after, she was seized, and when I left the group was still under detention. What steps were taken to return these people to their homes, I never heard. Here for the first time I saw the giant land crab that feeds on cocoa-nuts; these crabs are considered a great luxury by the natives. Such fearful strength are they possessed of, that there is only one way of keeping them safely, and that is by tying a cord round their waists and suspending them from the roofs of their houses. I being somewhat taller than the average of the natives, found my head several times in dangerous proximity to these animated chandeliers. The natives described to me a method of catching them, which I had often heard of before, but never really believed.

It appears that the crab is in the habit of climbing the cocoa-nut trees by night, and biting off a nut, which falls to the ground, when he immediately descends, clambering down backwards, to eat it at his leisure on the ground. Such being his custom, the natives outwit him by tying a wisp of grass round the stems of the trees at a great height from the ground. This the crab does not notice as he ascends, but in coming down backwards, as soon as he feels the wisp of grass he imagines he has reached the ground, lets go his hold, and falls to the bottom, where he is found in the morning by the owner of the tree.

Futuna and the smaller island Alofa were discovered as long ago as 1617, by two Dutchmen, Le Maire and Schouten, who first rounded Cape Horn, which owes its name to their birth-place. They were in search of the supposed great southern continent, but failing to find it, went on to Batavia. These islands were known to the Tongans, for we read in Mariner's work how Cou Moala, a Tongan chief, started on a roving expedition in the spirit of a knight-errant, and how he was driven by a gale to this place, where the people seized all he was possessed of, according to the custom of their country, some of the plunder was then offered to their gods, the remainder divided among the chiefs. However, when the strangers wished to depart, those who had shared the plunder were compelled to fit them out again.

The habit of plundering all shipwrecked strangers was also indulged in at Fiji, only that the strangers were generally eaten as well as plundered.

The appearance of the Futuna natives, their dark

colour and frizzly hair, would lead one to fancy that they were a mixed race of Fijians and Polynesians. It is a fact worthy of remark, that the name of the smaller island is Alofa; this is the word of salutation in Samoa. Alofa is the first of the two islands that a canoe would sight coming from Samoa; it might then have thus been named by them to express their joy at seeing land again.

On the 3rd of June we left Singavi Bay, and at daylight the following morning were off Uvea or Wallis Island, really a collection of small low islands surrounded by a coral reef. It fell calm and a canoe came off, with a very handsome old native, wearing a long white beard, who wished to act as pilot. The passage is only 120 yards wide, and the tide runs in and out, seven or eight miles an hour; it would have been madness therefore to attempt it without a good commanding breeze. I landed my blind passenger in the canoe, and we kept further off the land. By morning we were three or four miles off, and though not a breath of air was stirring, the sea was white with foam, and the noise of its ripples was like the rush of a rapid pebbly river. The current must be very strong. The weather looked unsettled, and with much reluctance I gave the order to head for Niuafoo. The wind shifted a little towards noon, giving us a fair wind for Samoa, so I determined to call in there; I had not originally intended doing so, not caring to visit islands so well known, and about which so much has been written from time to time.

On Monday, June 8th, we sighted Savaii, the largest island of the Samoan group, bearing east, distant about forty miles. Next morning we arrived off its south-west end; having had to beat against a head-wind. There is something very grand and majestic about this island, gradually and evenly sloping from the sea on all sides, till it ends in a peak over 5,000 feet high, which is always either hidden in or piercing through a dense stratum of cloud. And one cannot but feel some respect for it as being, if not the cradle of the Polynesian race, at least an island which has peopled, according to the natives' own account, some of the neighbouring islands; as being the island whence the Maories came, called by them Hawaiki, and whence too, in all probability, the distant islands of Erronan and Immer, in the New Hebrides, received colonists, which two islands now go by the names of Futuna and Niua respectively. Only the coast-line of this grand-looking island is inhabited; the long slopes from the shore to the summit consist of forest and tall grass, here and there broken up by small black-looking cones, which from the sea appeared to be extinct volcanoes. They say that the interior has never been penetrated by man.

At the south-west end of the island the coast is extremely rugged; there is no regular coral reef to protect it, but here the waves of the ocean are at ceaseless strife with the black volcanic rocks that form the shore. These dark masses are worn into deep caverns, into which the huge surf rolls, bursting out through cracks and blow-holes further on, like the spoutings of some gigantic whale.

We continued beating up close along this shore against a strong current, and next day, seeing what appeared a suitable place for anchorage, we sailed in, and dropped anchor in a large open bay, well sheltered from the trade winds. We were about half a mile from the shore, and the two extremities of the bay bore W. S. W. and N. N. E., the water of the bay being as smooth as glass. I mention our bearings, because I have not seen this anchorage mentioned in any chart or book of voyages.

There appeared to be a very large native town on the beach, and in a short time a boat came off with a white man, who, as is usual in these more civilized islands, was decidedly the worse for drink, and of whom I very soon got rid. We shortly afterwards lowered the boat and visited the shore, when we learnt that the name of the place was Safuni, and that Matatua, the only anchorage given on the chart, was some five miles further on. The people looked as clean and smart as Samoans are generally described, their heads thickly coated with white lime made them look like London footmen run wild. At the back of the town we found a large lagoon, the banks of which were thickly fringed with cocoa-palms, and a large fern much resembling our *Osmunda regalis;* amongst these here and there peeped out the neat white houses of the natives; we entered several of these houses, and found the inmates very friendly and chatty. I informed them I was anxious to buy provisions from them, and requested them to bring them off to the vessel, whither I returned shortly after in order to await their arrival. To my surprise no canoes came off, and I felt that there must have been some taboo placed upon my schooner. Next morning, however, the photographic party landed with the usual apparatus and staff of carriers. A crowd gathered round them on the beach, and very shortly afterwards canoes began to come off to the vessel. When I asked them why they had not come before, they told me that the white man on shore had persuaded them that I was a Fiji vessel come to steal men; in this way had our drunken visitor of yesterday endeavoured to avenge himself. I had a good laugh at them, telling them I was surprised that a civilized people like the Samoans could have believed such nonsense.

We now became very friendly, and the vessel was crowded from stem to stern, but unfortunately very little provision was to be got from them; they have been suffering from a long and lingering war, which has prevented them from attending to their plantations, and the soldiers had consumed all their pigs and fowls. These people are all nominal Christians under the London Missionary Society, but they seem to have profited but little, for I found they were arrant thieves, and their general morality was at the lowest ebb.

On the 12th we moved down the coast, and anchored in Mataatua Bay, and while the photographic party was engaged on shore, I endeavoured to get some provisions, of which we were now very short, but I had no great success. The next day therefore we moved on again, but met with much calm weather, and not till Sunday afternoon did we make the island of Upolu, and drop anchor in the harbour of Apia, which is the white settlement of the Samoan group.

The town is pretty and very pleasantly situated, but I cannot say that I brought away any pleasant reminiscences of the place.

No doubt, if one arrived there as a simple passenger without any responsibility, a visit might be made enjoyable, for the resident merchants are most kind and hospitable. Here, however, the greater part of my white crew gave me constant trouble.

The temptations offered to the British sailor at this place appear to be so great, that he forgets the respect due to himself, and runs riot in drink and debauchery. But there is no need for me to describe a place about which so much has been written; and it would require all the lime-light and spangles that an earl and a doctor could summon to make a truthful description of Apia at all presentable. Round the town is a considerable extent of flat or undulating country, but of course all covered with dense bush, well watered by streams of considerable size; this gives the settlers an opportunity of taking many nice rides or walks, a luxury not to be obtained on many South Sea islands. But it is melancholy to see the large area that has been laid waste by war; whole districts have been entirely cleared of their cocoa-palms and bread-fruit trees to build stockades and forts for the tribes engaged, and years must elapse before this part of the island recovers itself.

As I said before, I have no pleasant recollections of this place, and I was not sorry, though minus my captain and one of my crew, to get up the anchor and bear away for the island of Niuafu.

Soon after leaving the land, we passed through a school of whales, that appeared to be thoroughly enjoying themselves, tumbling and rolling about in a most undignified manner. The whole sea, too, was literally alive with fish. The bonita were leaping on every side of us, and a dense flock of terns and boatswain birds followed us, or, more properly speaking, the fish, all day long.

At daylight on the 20th we sighted Niuafu, which at a distance of fifteen miles has the appearance of three separate islands. At noon we were off the north-east end of it, and here I landed our ambassador from Rotumah. The word "landed" is hardly correct, for he had to jump out of the boat and swim to the rocks, there being a slight swell to-day which prevented the boat from approaching too near the shore.

Not knowing how long this fine steady weather might last, and consequently how long we could keep the vessel standing on and off the island (for it is impossible to anchor), I told the man before he left, that he had better come back the next day with some pigs if possible, although it was Sunday. The next day, however, the weather was still wonderfully fine, and no one appeared; we had therefore abundance of opportunity for examining the exterior of the island. The water is quite deep right up to the black rocks that fringe the shore, and we could sail close up to the land. The sea beats directly on to those black rocks, there being no coral reef whatever, so that in rough weather communication with the island is impossible, and even at the best of times one can rarely get on to the island without a ducking. Such being the disadvantages of the place, it is not surprising that the people are anxious to leave it for a more favoured island, such as Rotumah, when too, in addition to these external inconveniences, they have a volcano beneath them, which every now and then breaks out and destroys a whole village at a time. On Monday morning we stood close in and lowered the boat, to communicate with the shore. They pulled away to what appeared the likeliest place, and I saw a crowd of people come down to the rocks to meet them, bringing plenty of pigs and fresh provisions.

The getting of the pigs into the boat was very troublesome; a line had to be thrown ashore from the boat, a pig fastened to it, and then the poor wretch was drawn through the surf and lifted into the boat half drowned. Baskets of yams and cocoa-nuts were all sent off in the same way, payment being deferred till they could come off to the schooner to choose what they wanted. One trip of the boat occupied nearly the whole forenoon. In the afternoon the sea became much smoother, and some small canoes were launched from the shore, not a few of their occupants wanting me to take them away, but I refused in every case.

About 3 P.M. my boat was observed coming off from the shore, apparently very deeply laden, so we stood close in to save them a long row. We could see, too, that she had a great many natives on board.

On arriving alongside, men, women, and children scrambled up the side of the vessel and commenced handing up babies, boxes, and bundles of mats, and quietly seated themselves on the deck. I saw what all this meant. The people were bent on having a passage somewhere, and I suppose the Rotuman ambassador had painted in such glowing colours all the attractions of that island, that without hesitation they had decided to go there.

In a few minutes my vessel had all the appearance of an emigrant ship. At first I mildly suggested the impossibility of taking them, and informed them that I was not going straight back to Rotumah, but that I intended visiting several islands first. But this was no objection to them. Time was no object.

But I insisted on their getting into the boat and being rowed on shore, for unfortunately for me they had no canoes of their own to land in. Finding that they took no notice of me, and were not the least disposed to obey, for the men had quietly lit their pipes, and the women had commenced to suckle their babies, I ordered the bundles, chests, and children to be put into the boat, and then the men and women, looking reproachfully at me, slowly and reluctantly followed. I now expostulated with my boat's crew for bringing this crowd off. They had brought no more provisions of any kind and the whole afternoon had been wasted. They assured me they could not help it, for as the weather was fine and the sea very calm, they had been able to bring my boat close to the rocks. Taking advantage of this the natives made a rush on the boat, threw in their bundles and babies and jumped in, afterwards refusing to get out again.

The deck, however, was now clear. The Rotuman ambassador, his brother, and one child alone remained. Their wives I refused to take, and as the ladies were neither beautiful nor young, and not nearly so nice looking as the Rotuman dames, these young men at once agreed with me as to the impropriety of attempting to carry their better halves in a vessel without a ladies' cabin.

I had intended to sail away this afternoon, but the weather was so wonderfully fine, the sea being quite smooth, with just enough breeze to work the vessel easily, that I decided to remain by the island all night, and visit it myself in the morning.

The weather continued unchanged, and the sea was so smooth that I succeeded in landing dry-shod on some rocks about a mile and a half from yesterday's landing-place. We stept off the black rocks on to the richest volcanic soil, and in about ten minutes came on a straight well-kept road, carpeted with close soft turf, and bordered on either side by bananas, pine apples, and coffee plants, placed at regular distances. This led us through a large village, whence for some time I had heard a native Boanerges thundering out a prayer in a voice that might be heard all over the island. Just beyond the town we came on a regular village green, with its church, school, and burial ground, all in the most perfect order, and models of neatness. Then striking inland we had a very steep climb to gain the summit of the highest hill before us, in order to get a view of the lake that occupies the centre of the island. Half-way up we stopped to rest and the boys brought us fresh cocoa-nuts, for by this time the sun was getting powerful. Arrived at the summit, the view burst on one all at once. From our standing-point the mountain drops away almost precipitously for five or six hundred feet, but not so sheer as to prevent its being densely clothed with tropical vegetation. Beyond this, far below, and a little to the left, extend some bare low hills of black cinders, reminding one of pit hills in the coal districts; just beyond this lies the mysterious-looking lake, blue as a sapphire, everywhere but on the south-east side enclosed by perpendicular cliffs; there however the land falls away and forms as it were but a strip between lake and ocean. In the lake are two small well-wooded islets, on one of which the natives informed me was a spring of fresh water, the only one in Niuafu, the lake itself being brackish. It was truly a magnificent view, and we felt well repaid for our climb. The black wicked-looking cinder hills formed a striking contrast, and a not unpleasing relief, to the ever-green tropical vegetation of which after a time the eye must weary. No one sailing by this island, would imagine that a lake lay here so mysteriously hidden away in the mountains.

We sat some time here, and would gladly have stayed longer, but I did not know how soon a swell might get up on the sea, which might prevent our rejoining the vessel; as it was, we returned to the schooner as dry as we started.

Niuafu possesses cocoa-nuts that exceed in size even those of Rotumah. I have seen shells that would hold three-quarters of a gallon of water. Strange to say, here too is found a species of megapode, a small mound-building bird, which lays an egg of a brown colour, larger than that of a goose. This bird must surely have been imported at some time, for it is not found on any of the neighbouring islands, nor have I seen it anywhere nearer than the Solomon Islands, where they are very numerous. The eggs are most excellent, and are much prized by vessels engaged in the bêche-de-mer and pearl fisheries about Torres Straits. The young are able to fly immediately after they are hatched.

I managed to procure a live specimen, about the

size of a quail; he was very independent, and perfectly happy when I put him into a box with earth, which he at once commenced scratching about. Unfortunately, while I was at Fiji, a cat broke open the cage, and the bird flew on shore.

As we sailed round the southern and western sides of the island, we saw traces of recent volcanic outbursts, the country being quite black, and all vegetation utterly destroyed.

Before a strong and favourable breeze, we ran for the Fiji group. Taking warning, however, by Lord Pembroke's fate, we did not intend to enter this most dangerous group by the passage attempted by his vessel, but we kept well away to the south, with the object of coming into the group a little to the north of Turtle Island. As the sun sank, the wind freshened, and the night set in thick and rainy. At 4·30 A.M. I was roused from my bed, to which I had but just retired, by the cry of "Land ahead on the lee bow!" I rushed on deck, and stood shivering in the wind and rain, and saw the black loom of land through the mist and darkness, which unpractised eyes would never discover unless pointed out to them; and almost at the same time, more land was discovered in several directions. The only thing to be done was to bring the ship to the wind, and beat out in short tacks as near as possible by the way we had come in.

I felt no more inclination to sleep, but anxiously waited for the dawn. When at length the welcome daylight broke, we discovered land and reefs on all sides, and could now make out that we must have been swept out of our course by strong currents, though, no doubt, bad steering had a great deal to do with it. The nearest land to us proved to be Angasa, with its numerous small islets and coral reefs extending in all directions; whilst to the northward, several other small islands could be seen. We certainly had had a narrow escape.

There is no recognized entrance to the Fiji group in this direction, but my sailing master took up his position on the foreyard, and guided by him we sailed on, picking our way through reefs and shoals, past the islands Morambo and Kambara, and at 2 A.M. next day were close up to Matuku, where I intended anchoring.

The night was dark and rainy, with little wind, and again we had a narrow escape of going on the reef; the sea being so calm, that we could not make out the white breakers on the reef till we were almost on top of them. We just had room however to put the vessel round, and stood off the land till day began to break.

On arriving off the mouth of the harbour, we saw, to our great surprise, a large man-of-war anchored close under the land. We ran up our colours, and she showed the Italian flag.

The wind was blowing right off the land, and we waited for flood-tide before attempting to beat in. It was very ticklish work; the entrance was so narrow that at times we were not ten yards from the rocks as we went about. At length, however, we got past the extremely narrow part, and beating on, anchored about 200 yards inside of the frigate, in $17\frac{1}{2}$ fathoms.

Shortly after we had anchored, the captain of the frigate came on board, and complimented us on the "magnificent" way in which we had worked our vessel into the harbour through so narrow an entrance. I thanked him, and was delighted to think that my vessel should have kept up the credit of my nation in these distant seas.

The man-of-war proved to be the "Garibaldi" from Tasmania, bound to Japan. She had put in here to refit, while a surveying party was engaged in making a chart of the harbour. This seemed to me rather a work of supererogation, for it was accurately surveyed by Captain Denham of H. M. S. "Herald," in 1856. Perhaps, however, they had some reason, for the entrance has certainly narrowed much since Captain Denham's visit. He describes it as being one-eighth of a mile wide: "It led into a basin having sixteen fathoms of water, with swinging room for two or three frigates, and a shore well adapted for coaling, if ever deemed desirable as a dépôt for passing steamers." Strange to say, in spite of this recommendation, a harbour on the island of Kendavu, though much inferior to it, has been selected as the port of call for the mail steamers plying between the Australian colonies and San Francisco. The only reason for this is, that several of the more influential settlers in Fiji have bought land round the Kendavu harbour, and are anxious to improve the value of their property. Matuku, unlike Kendavu, is entirely free from outlying dangers, and is the most southerly island of the whole Fiji group; the dangerous network of coral reefs that is found about Kendavu does not here exist. I found provisions of all kinds most abundant here, and managed to lay in a good stock, giving the natives tobacco and calico in exchange for pigs, fowls, and ducks. The Italians were not provided with trade of this description, and could obtain no fresh provisions, for the natives did not care to accept money. I sent them therefore an interpreter and a supply of trade, and in a very short time they got as much as they wanted.

The scenery of Matuku is very beautiful, and our photographic party were busily employed. The whole island is broken up into high volcanic peaks, which have taken most fantastic shapes; but there appears to be very little land suitable for a cotton or sugar plantation. The natives appeared to be a dirty and inferior lot, living in filthy houses, which is very unusual for Fiji men. There were living amongst them a good many Tongans, who in every way evinced their superiority. I spent a very pleasant week here, making excursions on shore and about the bay, and got up fishing parties at night, when we always caught fish in abundance.

On the 8th of July we sailed out of the passage, and next morning arrived at Levuka. H. M. S. "Dido" was lying here, acting as a sort of guardian to British subjects in this miserable distracted little settlement. The country appeared to be in the most unsatisfactory condition; the small community being torn with dissensions. Nearly all the white residents seemed to be thoroughly disgusted with the mismanagement of Thakombau's self-constituted ministry. This ministry consisted principally of absconders from the various Australian colonies, and had, by flattering the old king, succeeded in arming and drilling a number of the natives, to keep the other white residents in subjection. They had managed to contract loans which they had no prospect of paying, and had flooded the place with so-called Treasury notes and I O U's, which were, to say the least, accepted with hesitation and suspicion.

On Friday, July 18th, Thakombau was received on board H. M. S. "Dido" with a royal salute, and the scene on deck was duly immortalized by my photographic party. Poor old king, what a guy they had made of him! Instead of his usual loose flowing robes of Fijian tappa, in which he looks every inch a king, his ministers had tricked him out in a close-fitting sky-blue jacket and flesh-coloured tights. I don't know where they got the idea from, but the result was a mixture of a London footman and a barrel-organ monkey. No one could have appeared to advantage in such a costume; but it was cruel and unfeeling to ask an old man over seventy years of age, who has one leg smaller than the other, from a spear wound, to make such an antic of himself.

In the evening, I rowed on shore with Captain Chapman of the "Dido," and found the old king sitting in front of his house on a fallen tree, with a fathom of cloth round his loins, smoking a clay pipe, in which costume he appeared far more at his ease, and much more of a king.

All this week my crew had been very busy cleaning the vessel thoroughly. Owing to the unpleasant smells on board, I had all the ballast taken out, thoroughly cleaned, and put back again.

On the 22nd I sailed for Vanna Balavu, an island on the eastern side of the group, and after a tedious passage of five days, for we were much delayed by calm weather, we anchored in Loma Loma Harbour on the 27th. This island has been occupied by Tongans, and here, as at Niuafu, they have made excellent roads. The original Fiji inhabitants seem to be quite in subjection to the Tongan chief, who now rules over all the islands on this side of the Fiji group.

I was most kindly and hospitably received by Mr. Levick, who is engaged in cotton planting here, and who did all in his power to make our visit a pleasant one, and our photography a success.

A few miles down the coast to the westward I was shown a cave full of bones. These were the remains of Tongans, who years ago had been overpowered and massacred by the Fijians, who appear to have endeavoured to resist the steady encroachments of their more enterprising neighbours from the Friendly Islands.

About a mile further on, we scrambled over some of the roughest volcanic country I ever saw, and came to a small cave filled with hot water. I should say the temperature was about 120°. It tasted very salt, and pieces of pumice stone were floating in it; but it was as clear as crystal, and afforded us some excellent bathing during our stay at the island.

On July 30th we sailed away round the eastern end of the island. The navigation was extremely difficult, for we were beset with reefs and shoals. At one place, where I thought we were in open water, the man on the foreyard cried out to me, "Look over the stern, sir." I did, and saw we had just passed over a sharp peak of coral rock, that appeared to rise in sugar-loaf form from the bottom of the ocean. Next day we made the island of Goro, but so heavy a gale came on that we were compelled to run before it and take refuge under a reef that runs off the northern end of the island. Here we were quite snug, and I went on shore and visited some of the cotton plantations on this most fertile island. The next day the weather moderated, and we sailed on to Levuka. I remained here only one day and then started for Rotumah, which island I reached on the 10th of August, and had the satisfaction of landing my lame little boy quite cured, and the two chief's sons in excellent health and spirits,—one of these latter wished to continue his voyage with me, but his father would not allow it.

The day after my arrival, I made arrangements with the chief of Noatau to hold a large fishing party, and early the following morning rowed up to that village in my boat. I found the natives all ready, awaiting my arrival, and as soon as my boat appeared off the village innumerable small canoes were launched from the beach. A larger one, containing the nets, put off from the canoe-shed opposite the chief's house.

These fishing parties always take place at half-tide. At high tide the water would be too deep for carrying on this style of fishing, and at low tide the fish go out into deep water outside the reef. At half-tide the water is about four feet deep. The nets are first fixed so as to form two sides of a triangle, the apex ending in a large bag net. Then hundreds of small canoes spread out, and, as it were, enclose nearly half a square mile of water; they then slowly advance, gradually closing in on all sides towards the net. The large canoe is stationed near the head of the nets, and in it the head fisherman stands directing the whole force, while here and there, standing in the water near the nets, are stationed some of the older men.

Almost as soon as the circle of canoes had commenced the advance, some of the more timid kinds of fish dashed into the net, and, unless there appeared a likelihood of their doing damage, they were allowed to mesh themselves.

In a very short time the circle of canoes had decreased to a quarter of its original size, and the fish, like a terrified flock of sheep, crowded into the net. Jokes, laughter, and good-natured chaff are the order of the day, for men, women, and tiny children all join in these big fishing parties. The splashing and shouting increases as the canoes approach the nets, and it is difficult for the head fisherman, who stands up frantically gesticulating in his canoe, to keep proper order in the advancing crowd. Many of the natives now leave their canoes and wade along, grasping a light fish-spear, and it is marvellous with what dexterity they will strike the fish that attempt to break back. When they have reached the two wings of the net, most of the natives jump into the water and advance in a compact line, so that the fish now have no choice but to hurry into the bag at the end of the net.

The dark forms of the natives are now seen diving about with the rapidity of seals, searching all the holes and corners in the rocks for lurking fish:

a great number which would otherwise escape are taken in this way, and when so captured are never appropriated, but always placed in the big canoe; not to do this would be considered an act of meanness. While the divers have been thus engaged, the bag net has been lifted into the big canoe, the fish taken out, and the nets made ready for another setting. The whole fleet then adjourns to another part, say half-a-mile away, where the same process is gone through again.

Four or five such hauls will usually supply sufficient fish to feed the whole town. After the final haul they adjourn to a flat rock on the shore, where the fish are laid out. Some of the better kinds are set aside for the chief, and the rest fairly portioned out by the head fisherman. Nothing can exceed the beauty of these fish. A haul of fish in England seems to consist of only half-a-dozen different kinds, but here one sees a collection of fish infinite in variety of form and colour. So grotesque are many of them in shape, so fantastic in their painting, that they are unlike anything else in nature, and seem rather the fanciful creation of some sportive fairy. One marvels at the extreme beauty of their colouring ; but their shapes are as a rule so excessively comical that it is impossible to look at them without laughing.

Owing to the state of the tide I had to wait some hours before returning to the vessel; unfortunately the weather became very violent, heavy squalls followed one another in rapid succession, and night closed on us while we were only half way to the vessel. The wind had by this time gone round to the north, so that when we got out of shelter of the reef we found rather a big sea running. The night was as black as pitch, and I could nowhere make out the vessel's light. Had I been sure she had gone out to sea, I would not have ventured to join her that night, but I was afraid they might have decided to wait for my return, so we rowed on. Sometimes, when mounted on the top of a big wave, we fancied we could see her light, but we were so soon in a valley between the seas that we could never be sure.

All at once I saw her under sail, close to us, and I was rather afraid we should be run down, but we all hailed her at the top of our voices, when she backed her topsail, and we got on board. This delay brought us in rather unpleasant proximity to the rocks, but we soon filled on her and stood off the land for the night.

The next day I shipped the remainder of my crew, for the four Rotumah boys that I had had with me wished to remain at home. I had now only two white men before the mast, and, I must confess, had about as nondescript and rascally-looking a crew as ever graced the deck of any pirate. To begin with, two natives of the Loyalty Islands, black as night, with woolly heads, and possessed of all the unfailing stock of mirth and apish tricks of the conventional stage nigger. Sam and Charlie were always a source of amusement to all on board. Next to these one Solomon Islander, anxious to go home, a thorough young scamp, but a hard-working boy. Then two natives of Rotumah, one from Rorotonga, and three from Ellice's group. These last six formed the lighter-coloured and more respectable-looking part of the crew. Later on I picked up two Spanish Malays, natives of the Philippines, Antonio Dilatori and Andreas Marsalas. This comprised my crew, and though they were all excellent fellows, and gave not the slightest trouble, yet I must say their appearance was against them, and a stranger would have been justified in hesitating to trust himself amongst such a nondescript ship's company.

What is the origin of that game with a piece of string, known to us as "Cat's cradle"? It is as general throughout the South Sea Islands as the cocoa-nut tree. I believe they play it at every island; but the shapes they produce are not so symmetrical as ours. They have names too for the various figures.

Nor is it a trifling game with them. I have watched grown-up natives playing it, and on one occasion two women were sent for, who, I was assured, were especially clever at it. These two set to work, and in about a quarter of an hour had produced a very complicated, but to my mind not very symmetrical figure, which was considered a triumph of art. But this was not all, movement by movement they worked back for another quarter of an hour, till the string was clear. In playing it they made much use of their mouths.

CHAPTER IV.

ON Wednesday, August 13th, I left Rotumah, bound for the New Hebrides, and at 2 A. M. on Sunday, land was sighted. None of us having ever visited these islands before, we waited for daylight, and then discovered we were off Traitor's Head, on the east side of the island of Erromango. This headland received its name from Captain Cook, on account of the treacherous character of the natives. The island of Tanna, for which we were bound, was visible to the southwards. For this latter we steered, but the wind fell and we did not get into Port Resolution till next morning. All night a volcano, which is situated about five miles north of Port Resolution, lit up the sky with a lurid glare; dark masses of smoke rolled up between us and the stars, while every now and then, with a sound as of distant thunder, showers of red-hot stones and ashes were thrown up to a vast height. At 7.30 A. M. we dropped anchor in Port Resolution. Nowhere are any native houses visible, but to our left, a little further up the bay, we could see the white house of the missionary, well situated on a bold bluff point that ended in black volcanic rocks. On our right, but scarcely to be distinguished from the morning mist, light columns of steam curled upwards from a number of boiling springs that bubble up amongst the shingle just at high-water mark. The volcano we had watched through the night was now hidden by the nearer hills that form the north side of the bay, though we knew its position from the occasional masses of black smoke that rolled up over the summits of the hills.

After breakfast we went on shore to call on the missionary. After visiting some of the missionaries on the Polynesian Isles, surrounded by their courteous inhabitants, with cleanly habits and good houses—after seeing the Wesleyan missionary in all his glory, monarch of all he surveys, head of an insular hierarchy, merchant, priest, and king—it is painful to see the position of some of the London

Missionary Society's ministers. I do not hesitate to say that, "come the three corners of the world in arms," and Tanna would shock them. The ordinary costume of these people cannot with propriety be described, nor hinted at. And here, now for some years, has resided a London Society's missionary. It is for him to say with what success he has met; at any rate, every unprejudiced person must admit that if he has not been successful, at least he cannot do any harm.

Up to the present time one cannot conceive that much improvement has taken place.

Ask that oiled and red-ochre-besmeared savage, in that indescribable costume which is worse than no clothing, if he is a Christian. He walks with a jaunty, defiant air, proud of his personal appearance, his flint musket thrown over his shoulder, and a feather stuck through the pierced septum of his nostrils. He may probably tell you he is a Christian; but, my friend, as long as thou comest in such a questionable shape I must refuse to believe it. All of them are tricked out alike, and amidst these foul caricatures of humanity resides a clergyman with his wife, and, worse than all, his children. It is impossible for them to preserve seclusion, it is impossible to prevent these gorillas from hanging round about the house. For the Melanesian lacks utterly the courtesy of the Polynesian; he is, and especially the Tanna variety, a merry, saucy, rude fellow; he and his tribe are against every one, and every other tribe is against his and against each other. In Polynesia the missionaries appear to have established a footing by gaining over some powerful chief or king to Christianity, who, in his turn, compelled his subjects to follow his example. Then followed intrigue, and the pressure of a man-of-war. The chief who was first converted became the most powerful on the island, and in a short time the whole island was Christianized. Here in Tanna no such opportunity exists, for each village is at war with its neighbour, and there is no one powerful chief to pick out as the instrument for introducing and extending Christianity. Truly, a life spent among these savages is the giving up all worth having in this world. This is indeed devotion to the Master's work. And it must be distressing to the missionary himself, possibly more so to his wife, to see their children of tender years, girls and boys, growing up in a villainous climate amongst such sights and sounds as these.

This state of things cannot be right. The almost hopeless task of Christianizing these savages should not be allowed to wither in the bud not only the tender bloom of youth, but the natural moral delicacy and innocence of children. Such a system as the present one is as a car of Juggernaut, under which these miserable little victims are crushed, and that too, not voluntarily, as in the case of the Indian fanatic, but they are cruelly thrown under its wheels by the well intentioned but too carelessly given subscriptions of English people.

We met the missionary near his house, and he kindly volunteered to take a walk with us. Guided by him we followed a path that wound along the south side of the harbour, a path overshadowed by some most magnificent and gigantic trees of the fig tribe; their branches were richly decorated by orchids and ferns, their trunks ornamented by bones of turtles, and pigs, and strings of beads, the votive offerings of the natives; the ground for some distance round them was quite bare of vegetation, and beaten smooth by the feet of the nightly dancers.

The vegetation of Tanna is luxuriant in the

extreme, and the soil in fertility excels Fiji. Yams here grow to an enormous size; I have seen some that would have been a good load for a man.

Occasionally we stopped in our walk to marvel at the beauty and variety of the crotons—they stood out like burning bushes in the otherwise unvarying green of the forest. Once or twice we came on the small hut and clearing of a native, fenced in by reeds, and quite isolated in the dense forest, for the Tanna people do not always collect in towns like the Polynesians. But never did we get a view of any extent through the dense forest, or over the tall rank grass, till we emerged on the summit of a bluff that overlooked the sea, and saw the distant island of Erronau looming bold and abrupt, like a fortress, from the ocean, in the heated air of noon; and away to our left the long low island of Immer, whose trees, just rising above the water, appeared from the effect of mirage, to have parted from the horizon and now floated quivering in the scorched air. By a winding path we descended to the sea shore, and bathed in a hot spring that welled up through the sand, and then returned by another native track to Port Resolution.

On our way we came upon a yam plantation, where a party of natives were supposed to be at work; they were now sitting down in a group, each had his musket by his side, and all were painted and besmeared with ashes, red ochre, and grease.

We asked them for some green cocoa-nuts, for our walk had made us thirsty, and offered them tobacco in exchange, but some time elapsed before one would take the trouble to oblige us, and when they did bring them they were rudely thrown in front of us unhusked.

A Polynesian would have been eager to offer his cocoa-nuts to a passing stranger, and then husk them and open them ready for drinking.

I had intended visiting the volcano next day, but the rain came down in torrents all night, and the morning broke heavy with frequent showers, and every hill-top was shrouded in mist. I therefore took the boat and went round to Sulphur Bay, a few miles north of Port Resolution. It lies nearly at the foot of the volcano. It was impossible to land here, for a heavy surf was rolling in upon the rock-bound shore, so we anchored just outside the breakers, and shortly after some natives came down, dexterously launched their canoes through the surf and came off to us. On my informing them that I wanted to buy pigs they went on shore promising to bring them, and we waited for them about an hour. In front of us the volcano continually hurled up stones and ashes, which I noticed rarely fell outside the crater, while strong jets of steam burst up from the sulphur-streaked cliffs on our left.

Miserable little wretches were the pigs when they did come, weighing about twenty pounds, with long snouts totally out of proportion to their bristly little bodies; however I bought all they brought, and then rowed back to Port Resolution. On regaining the vessel we found the two tribes on either side of the harbour engaged in war. As they were nearly all armed with muskets quite a brisk fire was kept up; there was a great deal of running to and fro and shouting and firing off muskets, which only concluded when night came on. I did not hear how many, if any, were killed or wounded.

While the battle was at its hottest, there were some of the natives on board the vessel selling bananas, who seemed utterly indifferent to the fight that was going on, scarcely caring to throw a glance towards the scene of the conflict. Indeed the Tanna men appear to engage in battle in much the same spirit that a lot of English boys would join in a snow-balling match.

The battle was not renewed next morning, and we sailed away for the island of Erromango, and anchored just at night-fall in Dillon's Bay, about five hundred yards from the mouth of a river.

Here, as at Tanna, no native houses were visible from the sea. This is a marked contrast to the Polynesian islands, where all the houses are built close on the sea shore, and are in full view of any vessel approaching the coast. But though no native huts could be seen, the white house of the missionary shone out conspicuous on the north bank of the river. Finding no canoes came off I rowed on shore after breakfast to call at the mission station. A crowd of natives met us and followed us up the rough shingly beach to the house. I certainly was not captivated with the appearance of these Erromangans. They are without doubt the ugliest and most disagreeable-looking natives I have yet seen. The Tanna people are ugly enough, but there is a jovial merry expression about their countenances which one cannot help liking. These people appeared lower in the scale of humanity, and there was none of the Tanna good-natured sauciness in their expression. Their costume, consisting of a few green leaves, is scarcely more decent than that of the Tanna natives.

The missionary was busily engaged in building his house, and it annoyed me to see a crowd of lazy savages sitting round watching him, and never offering to assist in any way. In hopes of getting some pigeons I had brought my gun with me, and now, accompanied by the missionary and two natives, I walked up the valley through which flows the river. It is a fine clear rocky stream, on either side of which rise the hills almost precipitously to the height of a thousand feet.

Shortly after leaving the mission house, we saw on the opposite bank of the river the graves of Mr. Williams, and of Mr. and Mrs. Gordon, missionaries, who were killed by these natives, and also the more recent grave of Mr. M'Nair, who fell a victim to this treacherous climate. And as my eyes turned from these graves to the living form of the present missionary, I could not help admiring the man who had stepped forward and filled the gap in the rank of these Christian martyrs. In our walk we met several natives of both sexes, who appeared to be as kindly-disposed as they were filthy. It is somewhat strange that here as well as at Tanna, where the men's costume is so wanting in decency, the women should be so well clothed. Here they wear a long petticoat of grass that fairly sweeps on the ground as they walk.

We looked into one or two of their wretched huts, which appear to be very carelessly built and are entirely open at one end. There were no mats to cover the bare earth, but in some we saw small bamboo stretchers raised about two feet from the ground, on which they sleep in order to avoid attacks of fever and ague, which are very prevalent here. Not seeing anything to shoot, and as there were apparently no pigeons in the valley, I proposed ascending one of the hills. The missionary went home, but I with the two natives commenced scrambling up the mountain side. We walked about for a long time, but had no sport. I only shot two doves, and by the time I had reached the valley again, was thoroughly fagged out and my clothes were torn to rags. In the afternoon, according to my request, the natives brought off their various weapons for sale, and I bought all that I could.

Though so inferior-looking a race they manage to make most excellent arrows and clubs. In buying a bundle of arrows one finds that hardly two of their elaborately-carved heads are alike. These arrows I found were called "fanné." This is undoubtedly a Polynesian word, it being used for arrows both in the Friendly Islands and at Rotumah. In Mariner's "Tonga Islands" is given a full description of the "fanné gooma," or sport of shooting rats with bow and arrow.

Finding that I had not come to Erromango to steal men, the natives became most friendly and were anxious to see every part of my vessel. This was not very pleasant, and I shall not be putting it too strongly when I say they stink. In order to see their skill in shooting arrows, I put up a mark, offering as a prize a piece of tobacco for the best shot, but I confess they did not betray any great excellence in shooting, nor could I discover that extraordinary accuracy of aim which is generally attributed to savages.

The clubs I purchased of them were of two kinds, the common sort they called "necrum." The better kind has a star-shaped head, this they called "delaomité." The star has eight points, and is most accurately cut. I also bought their combs made of bamboo and slightly ornamented, these they called "now." Flat wooden combs and single pins for sticking in their hair they called "nangasow." In addition to these I managed to get some of their stone tomahawks. The missionary told me they had also some white stone ornaments, much prized by them, but I failed to see or procure one.

I never saw so poor a people, no provisions of any kind were to be got from them, and this is the more extraordinary as they inhabit a very fertile valley down which flows a river teeming with large fish.

This afternoon there sailed into the bay the London Missionary Society's vessel, bringing two missionaries; she was bound home to Melbourne. One of the missionaries, with his wife and child, had just been brought off from the neighbouring island of Espíritu Santo, which he was compelled to leave on account of the hostility of the natives. These wretches, in hopes of plunder, attacked his house at night. He told me he was sitting with his child in his arms, when several spears came through the grass walls of his house. With considerable presence of mind he blew out the light, and seizing an axe, chopped a hole in the wall, and through this opened fire on them with his gun. The cowardly savages immediately bolted. The missionary gave me to believe that he fired with blank cartridges only.

Some months afterwards I was in Auckland, when this story was told from the platform of a missionary meeting, terribly garbled to suit the ears of a missionary-meeting audience. The plucky missionary was represented as offering no resistance to the savages, and held up to the sympathizing audience as a helpless martyr. It is a grievous pity that any speaker on behalf of an excellent society should think it necessary to try and raise subscriptions by the sacrifice of truth.

Next morning, accompanied by two natives, I climbed one of the neighbouring mountains and had a good view over land and sea. Over the mountains that stretched away inland I saw much fine undulating table-land covered with grass, and apparently quite uninhabited. The boys that accompanied me brought me some twigs of sandal-wood, for which this island used to be famous, but which is now almost extinct. Horrible atrocities were committed by Sydney traders in years gone by, to procure this sandal-wood. For rather than open up legitimate trade with the natives, and pay them a fair price, they would arm a large body of natives from other islands, not unfrequently from Rotumah, and send them on shore to cut the sandal-wood and shoot down all resisting natives. This sandal-wood when procured was shipped to China, it being largely used there as incense.

The summit of the mountain was a bare flat rock, on this I sat and enjoyed the sea breeze; my schooner lay at anchor in the bay in front of me, and I could see the photographic party, winding away along the banks of the river, with its usual procession of tents and cameras, full 1,500 feet below. While seated here I could not but admire the dexterity of my two companions, who amused themselves by breaking off all the straight saplings that grew within their reach, and with apparently a few strokes of their knives carve on them an excellent and symmetrical barbed arrow-head, which as soon as made was hurled, spear-fashion, down the side of the mountain. When they found that I was watching them, and taking an interest in their work, they vied with one another in making more elaborate heads to these shafts, but it seemed to cause them no effort of eye or brain. The hand that held the knife descended without hesitation on the right spot, and the arrow-head was always completed without bungling. In the evening I just landed for a short time to wish our missionary friend good-bye and then sailed away for the island of Vaté, the next of the New Hebrides that lay in our route. With the first glimmer of dawn we could distinguish the remarkable hat-shaped island that forms an excellent guide to the entrance of the principal harbour on the island of Vaté. In the uncertain light it appeared the exact image of a cardinal's hat. Leaving this to our left, we entered Havannah Harbour, so named by Captain Erskine of H. M. S. "Havannah," who visited it in 1849. The entrance is free from all dangers, and we passed on, full sail, up this magnificent inlet. The shores on either side consist of moderately high undulating country. Here and there we saw the houses of white settlers, standing in patches of cleared land, now planted with cotton.

After proceeding five or six miles up we dropped anchor opposite what might almost be called the town. In the United States it would be dignified with the name of city. Here on the beach stand five or six white men's cottages, and near them is a steam cotton-ginning establishment, and a mill for working cocoa-nut fibre, also driven by steam, while for some distance all round the jungle has been cleared off and the land planted with cotton, which appeared to be growing most luxuriantly. A few hundred yards from us lay another vessel at anchor, which proved to be from Fiji and was in search of " labour."

At daylight next morning, I rowed two miles down the harbour to the missionary's house, for I had brought letters and parcels for him from his fellow-worker in Erromango. It was a lovely morning, and at that hour the air was most exhilarating. The water was as clear as crystal, and I steered close in shore, under the shade of magnificent trees that overhung the bank. They were a perfect mass of flowering creepers, and flocks of pigeons and parrots were fluttering about in the branches overhead, busily engaged in devouring the berries. Every now and then we startled a turtle from the banks; they were always too quick for us, and swam with rapid strokes through the clear shallows, till where the water deepened they gradually faded from view, many fathoms below us, and finally disappeared in the deep blue water of the harbour.

Arrived at the mission-house, it was some time before I could rouse his reverence, who, when he did appear, looked anything but pleased at being pulled out of bed so early. I delivered my parcels and letters, and rowed home to breakfast, leaving our friend yawning and stretching, and rubbing his eyes. After breakfast we cruised about the harbour, exploring all sorts of holes and corners, and following creeks that ran up for miles through the most dismal mangrove swamps, that looked as if they ought to be full of alligators, but are only inhabited by swarms of small crabs, that rapidly disappeared into little round holes whenever the boat approached them. There was nothing to shoot, and no scenery worthy of the camera. Nature seemed to have expended her forces in the production of fish, the water in these mangrove swamps being literally alive with fish of all sizes.

Later in the day, I went down the harbour in hopes of being able to get some of those pigeons or parrots that I had seen in the early morning, but I was disappointed, not one was to be seen; and, no doubt, during the heat of noon they had taken refuge in some dense shady jungle far inland.

The white residents here seem to think a good deal of their rising settlement, and assured me they were anxious to have a resident consul. It is evident that a second Fiji is springing up here, and that with its growth, will spring up the same abuses, the same native difficulties, and the same irregularities, not to say outrages, in the procuring of labour for plantations. This offshoot of the colonies should therefore be taken in hand in time. The child should be trained up in the way it should go, as a credit, and not a stain upon the English nation. It would be worth while trying if it were possible to colonize one place in the earth without destroying the aboriginal race, that is of itself utterly incapable of resisting the attacks of grog and European garments.

The natives of Vaté, though they will not work for planters here, have been taken in large numbers to Fiji, where they prove to be excellent labourers. The settlers on Vaté are compelled therefore to procure their labour from other islands. It follows, then, that the system of getting labour which we have endeavoured to regulate in Fiji, exists here, free from all restraint, but for the occasional visit of a man-of-war. I must however do the planters the justice to say, that all the labourers I saw looked fat, happy, and contented; in fact, much improved by transplantation from their own savage islands.

The natives of Vaté had little in the way of trade to offer. The presence of the white man has already had its effect upon them. They will be rapidly reduced to the condition of paupers; all that they can produce being without doubt squandered at the grog shop which is attached to one of the planters' residences. This is much to be regretted, for the Vatese really are a remarkably fine race.

The settlement in Havannah Harbour will, no doubt, develop itself rapidly. There is an abundance of splendid land, well adapted for either sugar or cotton; and, though the natives will not work, plenty of labour is to be had from the neighbouring islands. The climate is said to be not so healthy as that of Fiji. Fever and ague is very prevalent, and hurricanes and earthquakes are by no means uncommon. The natives are not so dark as the Tanna people, and are altogether a superior-looking race. Though they lack the wild and ferocious appearance of some of their neighbours, they are nevertheless treacherous and revengeful; and even within the last few months they have attacked and massacred crews of vessels visiting the island.

It is true these vessels were engaged in the labour traffic, and that wholesale kidnapping has been practised here; so that those who suffered at the hands of the natives, always richly deserved it. The houses of the Vatese are far superior to those on any of the neighbouring islands. There is nearly always a staging erected in the house, under which fires are kept constantly burning, in the smoke of which they sleep, by this means avoiding the attacks of the mosquitoes.

At daylight next morning I discovered to my dismay that my cook, George Robertson, had run away in the night. This was a blow that was felt by everyone on board, for in this out-of-the-way place it was of course impossible to replace him. He had never been a favourite on board, yet I must confess we never knew how much we loved him until we had lost him.

There were yet some hours before breakfast-time, so I hurried on shore with the object of recovering him, if possible, in time to prepare our usual morning meal; but I searched in vain for him and could hear nothing of his whereabouts.

One of the planters was most kind in making enquiries amongst the natives; and what is more, placed at my disposal about one hundred natives of other islands, who formed his plantation hands. These men were to go and scour the bush in search of the absconder.

To this body of savages I made promises of large rewards of tobacco and knives if only they would find him, and they, thoroughly entering into the spirit of the chase, opened out in line, and commenced to search the jungle. I was much amused by my planter friend, who kept impressing on his men that if they found the cook, they were to bring him like a sinner, every sentence of his "pigeon English" ended with "you bring him all the same like sinner." On enquiry I found that they had picked up the word "sinner" from the missionaries, and that the term had now come to be used in a conventional way for anything bad. Thus a bad cocoa-nut or a rotten yam is a sinner cocoa-nut or a sinner yam. In this case it implied that the natives were to tie my cook hand and foot and bring him home, they were not to be afraid of him because he was a white man, but to treat him as a sinner.

The loss of our cook was deeply felt by all of us, especially about breakfast time; still there was something very ludicrous in sending out natives to hunt for him in the bush, so ludicrous that it actually extracted a joke from the brain of my very Scotch sailing master, who remarked that he had often heard of Cook discovering savages, but never before of savages discovering a cook. I never knew him make more than that one joke. The savages, however, did not discover Cook in this case—he had successfully baffled his pursuers, and they all returned looking somewhat disappointed. One of my two white sailors consented to try and do our cooking for us, if we would not expect too much of him. A Rotumah boy was told off to him as scullery maid, and we sailed out of the harbour.

At night the volcano on the island of Ambrym was in violent eruption, and though it was at least sixty miles away, the air was filled with fine ashes, and everything on deck was covered with a grit resembling gunpowder. It penetrated into the cabins; eyes, nose, and mouth were choked with it, causing terrible irritation.

Fortunately the weather was very fine, and in the direction of the volcano the whole heaven was lit up with a wild lurid glare, that might have been mistaken for an aurora, only that at times it glowed with greater brilliancy.

The following day we sailed into a bay on the south-east side of Mallicolo, discovered by Captain Cook, and called by him Port Sandwich.

It was curious to see the natives behaving in exactly the same way as they did when the great explorer visited them. To-day, just as he describes it, crowds of people were on the reefs at the entrance of the bay, apparently engaged in fishing, or picking up shell-fish. None of them appeared to take the slightest interest in the stranger vessel that passed at no great distance, and when we had entered the harbour, and dropped anchor opposite a sandy beach, only a few natives came down to look at us. There was no waving of green boughs, or other signs usually made by islanders to induce one to land; they only stood in a group on the sandy beach, and looked at us in silence, all armed with bows and arrows, clubs and spears. I, however, had made up my mind I would go on shore and endeavour to open up friendly communications with them, and, knowing what a wild distrustful set of savages I had to deal with, determined to land alone.

I believe that everyone on board would have been willing enough to land with me, but I felt a heavy responsibility resting on me, and if anyone had suffered through my asking them to accompany me on shore, I should never have forgiven myself. The small boat was manned by a white man and a native of Maré, and having collected some beads, looking-glasses and tobacco, I was rowed towards shore. As soon as the water was shallow enough I stepped out of the boat and waded towards the beach. There was no sign of warning or of greeting from the group of about forty natives collected on the beach, and I felt by no means sure of what would happen next. However, I waded on towards them, endeavouring to look as pleasant as I could under such awkward circumstances. When I had got pretty near the beach each held an arrow ready on the string of his bow, and as I walked forward so they walked backwards from me, but as I gradually overtook them they walked away in different directions, so that I found myself at last in the position of the blind-folded member of a game of blind man's buff. If I approached one native he would slink away as if fearful of my touch, when I would advance towards another, and so on. Finally I just touched one, and he motioned me to sit down. This I did, and in a minute they all gathered round me and sat down too.

I now tried to open up conversation, and asked them to bring me cocoa-nuts or yams, in every language that I knew, but to no purpose, they would not or could not understand me. Some of those sitting nearest began to feel my clothes, and then, growing more familiar, felt my bare arms, and especially the palms and backs of my hands, uttering a clucking sound at the same time, expressive of admiration. The palm of the hand is considered by cannibals to be the most delicate morsel.

This habit of feeling one over and clucking might, of course, be their way of paying a compliment. Perhaps, amongst them it may be the politest thing in the world to say to another, " What an excellent feed you would make!" just as we should say, " How well you are looking!" However, it is, I must confess, anything but pleasant to be treated in this way.

When they were tired of this they wanted to pull out my revolver, but this I would not allow, and, pointing to their poisoned arrows, made signs to them that as their arrows would kill me, so my pistol would terminate their existence. I felt anything but sure of my position, for no women or children were visible—an unmistakeable sign of fear or hostility. I saw too that I could not open up friendly communications with such a lot of savages, and determined to leave them. The thing was how to get away, for I was afraid the first movement on my part might be misconstrued, and taken as an act of timidity or treachery, so I resolved to rise to my feet with all the sang-froid I could muster. I now heard drums beating away up in the bush, which of course was a signal for something, so I drew from my pocket a small looking-glass, and gave it to one man in exchange for his club, gave another a few beads, slowly rose to my feet, and sauntered down to the beach. This was the most anxious time of all. The natives at once followed in a crowd jabbering noisily, and I was prepared to feel at any moment an arrow sticking in my back. Every now and then I turned round and gave some man a few beads in exchange for some trifle. Seeing this, they grew very clamorous, and several times things were snatched from my hands, at which I could only look pleasant, as if I had been accustomed to that sort of treatment all my life; and, discretion being the better part of valour, I gradually gave them all the trifles I had about me. I then made signs that I had nothing more, and told them to stop, signing to them that I would return and give them more. Thus I told them a deliberate lie, believing that they would not kill me as long as they thought anything was to be got out of me. I was very glad to get into the boat and regain the vessel, when I gave the order to get up anchor and go out. It may to some appear cowardly that I allowed myself to be insulted by a set of savages. But what was to be done? How could one resist? Nothing but the use of firearms would have had any effect, and I was not disposed to shoot at a poor ignorant savage because he stole from me a small looking-glass or a string of beads. I confess, however, that I did not feel at all kindly-disposed towards them, and should be delighted to see them all kidnapped, and hard at work in some Fiji cotton plantation. This would no doubt have a most beneficial effect on them; three or four years of discipline, with regularity of work and meals, would open their minds considerably, and pave the way for better things. Up to the present nothing has been done with them, every attempt has failed. It is a shame that so magnificent an island as Mallicolo should be occupied by a lot of noxious savages.

Captain Cook describes them as being the most hideous and ape-like race he had ever met. From what I saw of them, I cannot say that they are any worse than the natives of Erromango; if anything, they were rather better looking, though their big heads of hair, and their habit of piercing the septum of their nostrils, does not add to their personal appearance.

I noticed that they covered themselves in the same way as the natives of San Christoval, in the Solomon group. Mallicolo was known by name as long ago as 1606. The Spanish navigator Quiros was told of it by the natives of Tucopia, a small island lying three or four degrees further north.

After leaving Mallicolo we passed a horrible night, the weather as the sun set was wild and stormy, and it became as black as pitch, with violent squalls of rain; at one time we were going ten knots through the water, at another tossing about helpless without a breath of wind. Land was all round us, inhabited by a pleasing variety of cannibal savages; and, added to this, the sea was more phosphorescent than I have ever known it. Lightning was flying round us, followed by thunder that seemed to shake the vessel; we had that extraordinary luminous appearance at the masthead, which was known in old days as a *corpo santo ;* and three different volcanoes, whenever the weather lifted, were distinctly visible in violent eruption, filling the air with fine ashes that were most painful to the eyes. We were glad, however, to get an occasional glimpse of these volcanoes lighting up the sky, for they enabled us to keep our position, and gave an assurance that we were not drifting in the calms, or being driven by the violent squalls, on to some unseen reef or rocky coast. It was truly a night of infernal horrors, and daybreak brought relief to all on board.

The following evening we were off Cape Lisburn, the south-west extreme of the island of Espiritu Santo. The day was nearly done and we did not venture to stand in close and find an anchorage, for the weather looked very uncertain. It was just as well we did not, for the sun set in a wild looking bank of clouds, our south-east trade-wind fell altogether, and then we had a succession of squalls from the north-west.

Not caring to spend the night on a lee shore, we hauled off the land a mile or two, and then stood northwards along the coast under easy sail. This island is far the largest of the New Hebrides, and its appearance from the sea is very grand. Peak rises beyond peak, the interior from its broken nature reminding one of the south-west coast of New

Zealand. Surely here, if anywhere, one might look for a pure aboriginal race. To some of these rugged highland districts the primitive inhabitants would have betaken themselves, when driven from the coast by an invading race, and here, from the difficult nature of the country, they would have been able to keep themselves independent of any encroaching power. I longed to be able to penetrate some of these lonely valleys or climb these virgin peaks. The sun as it went down lit up the mountains with golden tints, and I felt that the old Spanish navigators, coming upon this land after traversing a weary waste of water, were not to blame in thinking that here at last they had discovered the great southern continent, the Terra Australis Incognita that they were in search of.

In 1606 Quiros anchored in a bay on the north-east side which he called the bay of Vera Cruz, at the same time christening the island as Terra Australis del Espiritu Santo.

He reported this discovery to his sovereign in glowing colours, begging him to take possession of it. But it appears that he was led by his enthusiasm to overstep the bounds of truth; for Torquemada, who wrote an account of his voyages, says, that "from Espiritu Santo they set sail, desirous of discovering the lands to windward, to found other cities in honour of His Majesty, as had been done in this bay, where they founded one named New Jerusalem, to which were named alcades, regidores, royal officers, and other ministers of justice."

Now, considering that Quiros arrived at this place on the 3rd of May and left it on the 5th of June, it is scarcely likely that they had time to build a town. I have made particular mention of this, because stone ruins do actually exist on the north-east end of the island, the origin of which is unknown to the natives.

These, however, can scarcely be attributed to the Spaniards. They only lay here a month, and had they pretended to build a town it would not have been made of stone. For example, eleven years before, in 1595, Mendana and Quiros commenced a settlement on the island of Santa Cruz, and of this they give an account. We are told that the Spaniards stayed there two months and ten days, and then re-embarked, the natives being so hostile, and their commander Mendana having died. They further relate that " the soldiers with great alacrity cut down trees, bringing sticks to make huts, and palm and other branches to cover them ; forgetting their labour, and the little pleasure they then enjoyed, and thought no more of their native country, nor of having left Peru, so rich and extensive: all the difficulties which could offer they surmounted, for the service of God, and for that of their king. In short, they built their houses and fitted out their shops, each in the best manner he was able, to begin what they were to finish by degrees, where they intended to live and die with honour and fame."

I was sorry not to be able to visit the ruins on Espiritu Santo, but I was now getting short of fresh provisions, and despaired, after so many failures, of getting any amongst the New Hebrides. In addition to these we found a Queensland vessel on the coast engaged in the labour traffic, and it occurred to me, that if any native had a grievance, or had felt himself wronged either in that vessel or in Queensland, he would be very likely to try and get satisfaction out of me. So I reluctantly gave the order to bear away for the Solomon Islands.

CHAPTER V.

WITH a fresh fair breeze we bore away for San Christoval, and soon left the Terra Australis of Quiros far behind, an island which remains in as savage a condition, and scarcely better known than when the old navigator discovered it nearly two hundred and seventy years ago.

Our good fair wind kept with us, and at noon on Sunday, August 31st, we sighted Cape Surville, the extreme eastern point of the island of San Christoval. But when we got within five miles of the land, the strong trade-wind that had brought us thus far failed us suddenly without any warning, and left us tossing in a troubled sea, without a breath of air. Thus we lay till after sunset, when a breeze came off the land, and we sailed on westwards down the coast, and by daylight found ourselves off the entrance to Makira Bay, where I intended anchoring. As the sun rose so the land-breeze, that had helped us all night, became weaker and finally failed us altogether, when we were left becalmed for an hour or so. This seems usual amongst these islands. The large and lofty islands of this group interrupt the regular oceanic trade-winds, and in their place give one a sea-breeze during the day, a land-breeze during the night. Makira Bay was at once recognized by the Solomon Island boy I had brought from Rotumah, and with the first light breath of the sea-breeze, we stood in towards the entrance.

As we sailed slowly down the open bay, which gradually contracts and forms the entrance to Makira harbour, we could see numbers of canoes paddling about close in shore; but they appeared very shy and would not come near us till we had almost entered the harbour; then, as we drew slowly in with a light breeze, they came nearer and paddled round us in their canoes. These are unlike anything we had yet seen in the South Seas, and are perfect gems of beauty. At both ends they rise in a graceful curve to a sharp peak, so that the frail little craft has the appearance of a crescent lightly resting on the water. The outrigger so generally used throughout the Pacific islands is lost sight of here, except in the case of the very small canoes, which they use for paddling about the inner harbour. These latter are very tiny, being sometimes only ten inches wide, and their outrigger consists of the stem of a cocoa or sago-palm branch. They are more crank than any outrigger sculling boat in England, and it requires considerable skill to sit them; they were a constant source of amusement during our stay here, some of us were for ever paddling about in them, and generally met with a speedy capsize.

When the harbour, which is completely land-locked, opened out, we turned the schooner sharp round a rocky point to the left, and anchored in eight fathoms close in shore, for the water here deepens very rapidly; just facing us was the principal village of the bay.

The whole scene was like one in a fairy tale, for when the ripples caused by our casting anchor had died away, the multitude of tiny canoes that had followed us in, still floated half distrustfully around us, and each frail little vessel, with its swarthy occupants, lay perfectly mirrored in the glassy water of the bay. Every palm tree on the beach was reflected in the water, that only now and then betrayed its imperceptible heavings by lazily lapping the coral beach.

The scant air that had brought us in still rustled in our unfurled topsails, but failed to reach the water, so closely sheltered were we by the wooded hills that fringed the harbour; only out in the centre of the harbour, light eddying puffs ran here and there, ruffling the surface of the water, and then suddenly dying. We only had just time to take in the scene before the canoes, gaining courage, came alongside, and their dusky occupants climbed on board.

We now found ourselves amongst a people utterly unlike any of the islanders further south. Small in stature, though strongly built, and of very dark hue, the native of San Christoval is not while young actually hideous, but this is all that can be said for his personal appearance. He wears not the dignified appearance of the Fijian, nor the wild savage independent look of the New Hebrides native. He is passionately fond of ornament, and while wearing scarcely any covering at all, he loads himself with decorations. His arms are covered with heavy white rings made from the huge tridacna, he ties a coronet of white cowries round his temples, and sticks a long comb in his almost woolly hair, to which he also delights to attach a large scarlet tassel of grass. In his nose he wears a large ring of either tortoise-shell or mother-of-pearl; has neatly plaited anklets of dyed grass, and invariably slings from his naked shoulders a small bag in which he keeps little odds and ends, such as fish-hooks made of pearl shell, or a spoon of the same material; invariably he has with him a neatly engraved bamboo box containing lime, and this he uses to mix with the betel-nut which he incessantly chews from morning to night. In addition to all this some of the more important men wear a large crescent of mother-of-pearl suspended on their chest, on which they set a very high value and which they cannot be induced to part with at any price. These were the people who now crowded on board my schooner, and it seemed strange indeed to be accosted by them in one's own language; but the fact is the harbour was at one time occasionally visited by whalers, and some of the men have been tempted to go for a cruise; one or two that I met had paid visits to Sydney and Hobart Town.

Soon after anchoring King Wasinow came on board, neatly dressed in a straw hat and a shell bracelet, and as he spoke a few words of English, I got on very well with him, and promised to commence buying yams and general fresh provisions from his people the following morning. He then told his subjects that everything they brought on the following day would be purchased by me, and shortly afterwards went on shore.

In the afternoon, taking my gun, I rowed down the harbour, Mr. Smith accompanying me to look for subjects for the camera, and in addition to my own South Sea Island crew I took two natives of this place to show me where pigeons were to be found.

As we have travelled north and west over the Pacific, so does the climate appear to have become moister and warmer, and as a consequence the vegetation is more luxuriant. Here, as we landed from the boat, it was truly magnificent. The forest trees, with long straight stems, towered to a vast height above the cocoa-nut, sago, and areca palms; with these latter were mingled gigantic tree ferns, often attaining a height of thirty or forty feet. Of course the atmosphere in such a forest is steamy and oppressive. It is pleasant enough to sit down and look at nature so grandly dressed, but walking about with your chin in air looking upwards for pigeons will generally be found a mistake. The countless vines and perfect network of creeping plants are for ever entangling one's feet. And whilst in pursuit of pigeons the unwary sportsman constantly finds himself in the position of Andrew Marvel in the garden :—

> "Stumbling on melons as I pass,
> Ensnared with flowers I fall on grass."

We however scrambled up the first range of hills, but finding no view was to be had in any direction, returned at once with a few pigeons to the boat. The two Makira lads that accompanied me, professed to be very anxious at my going even as far as I did, giving me to understand that there were people living up in these hills who were not to be trusted. We now continued rowing round the harbour, occasionally shooting pigeons that stupidly sat in the trees overhanging the water. We presently passed by a small wooded islet. Here they told me they deposit the bones of their dead after separating them from the flesh. This appears to be the custom, for I was shown another bare rocky islet near the entrance of the harbour used for the same purpose. The bones of chiefs are, however, collected and placed in the large canoe shed, near their own canoe. A similar custom is described by Lord Byron as prevailing in the Sandwich Islands. "As soon as Kamehameha's death was ascertained, he was placed in a canoe on a thick bed of leaves, and he was also covered with leaves, that the flesh by being heated might become sufficiently soft to separate easily from the bones; as soon as that had taken place it was removed with wooden saws and carefully burnt. The bones being cleaned were then wrapped in a war cloak, and placed in the tomb house, where they were venerated by the people and especially by his family."

I had noticed as we entered the harbour in the morning, that there were villages perched on the summits of the different hills surrounding the bay, and now as we rowed round the harbour, we passed a path that apparently led almost precipitously up to one of these villages. Here a number of natives came out, making signs to us to land. My two native guides would not, however, hear of this, declaring that these men meant mischief. My own opinion of the matter was, that my guides were simply jealous of my having anything to do with another tribe, fearing that some of my trade might pass into their hands, and that this was the sole reason of their begging me not to go near these fellows. However, I yielded to them, and despite the solicitations of those on shore, continued rowing round the harbour. When we had arrived at the village that faced our anchorage, I stepped on shore.

The Solomon Islander's house is far more substantially built than the average Polynesian house; the walls are constructed of split bamboo, sometimes doubled, to make them spear-proof; the rafters of the roof are also made of large bamboo stems, and the whole is surmounted by a thatched roof of sago-palm branches. The eaves of a Polynesian house almost touch the ground, and as a rule, the ridge-pole runs parallel to the frontage. In the Solomon Islands the houses have good bamboo walls, that raise the eaves seven or eight feet from the ground, and the gable end always forms the front of the house. To enter it is necessary to mount a small verandah of bamboo, raised about three feet from the ground, and then, passing through a small square doorway, descend to the level of the ground again inside.

In fact, the entrance to a Solomon Island house is formed like the pigeon-holes of a dove-cote. The houses are always dirty, and it appears strange that a people so clever at all kinds of plaiting and weaving, should not take the trouble to weave mats for the floors of their houses. With the exception of a few miserable little scraps of very coarse matting, I never saw any covering to the floor; the natives sleep on the bare earth.

I have sometimes seen an attempt at divisions in the interior of a house. I do not know whether this is an idea taken from the white man; but what greatly assists the appearance of untidiness and dirt, is their habit of storing up heaps of yams and other produce in their houses.

The chief objects of interest in every village are the canoe houses. These are long sheds open at both ends, with the exception of a low palisade to keep the pigs out. In these sheds are kept the big canoes, which appear to be the property of the tribe. The roof is supported by a number of posts, each post being a human figure, half life-size, standing on a pedestal. Some of these figures have elaborately carved head-dresses, and all have represented on them the ornaments worn by natives at the present day. In fact, with the exception that they are quite nude, and have these extraordinary head-dresses, carved to receive the beams of the roof, they are exact representations of the present race of natives. No two of these figures are the same, although the same set of figures is repeated in all the canoe sheds that I visited. It would appear from this that they are stereotyped forms, recognized by tradition, possibly the effigies of some hero or god, and apparently emblematic, for each figure holds something in his hand, such as a fish, or a paddle of a canoe. At the present time the people do not look on them with superstitious awe. In answer to my enquiries they called them " A'öo," which, I should imagine, corresponded to " Atua," the general name for god or spirit throughout Polynesia.

The greater part of the shed is occupied by the large canoes, capable of holding at least twenty men. They have no outrigger, and rise to a high peak at both ends. They are richly carved, and tastefully inlaid with white shells and mother-of-pearl. I saw one specially fine canoe, of which the natives appeared very proud. Each thwart consisted of a fish, carved in dark wood, and inlaid with mother-of-pearl; its high stem and stern were decorated with scarlet tassels, and coronets of the snow-white *Cypræa ovula*.

In these sheds too are seen the wooden gongs for summoning the people to feast or war, huge wooden cylinders in which they pound up their food, and numbers of small and often elaborately carved wooden bowls. The roof is literally covered with the jaw-bones of pigs and dogs, and the heads of porpoises and cow-fish; and what is more highly prized, rows of human skulls. These grim mementos of their cannibal feasts contrast strangely with the graceful and highly decorated canoes.

There was at first a mystery about some wicker-work cases raised on poles by the side of some of the canoes, but I found out that these cases contained the bones of chiefs once the owners of the canoes near which the remains were placed. Here they told me they placed the bones, looking on them as still owning the canoe, which is never launched again.

In these sheds, too, take place the public feasts. On these occasions, the wooden bowls that lie about the shed are filled with a curious mixture of yams, bread-fruit, taro, and cocoa-nut pounded up together; on the top of this they pour cocoa-nut oil, and garnish the whole with betel-nut.

These feasts, of which I have seen several, looked very pretty when laid out in the shed, but it is well not to go too near. Fermentation takes place rapidly in this climate, and the odour is anything but pleasant. They do not eat it until it is well fermented, and then I am told the preparation becomes somewhat intoxicating.

Their dances are unlike anything in the other South Sea Islands, and more resemble a Spanish fandango. When dancing, they tie bunches of hollow nut-shells on their wrists, which give out a sound something like castanets. May not this dance have been taken from the Spaniards who first discovered these islands in 1595? At the conclusion of a dance, I noticed a peculiar ceremony. An old man held up a freshly-husked cocoa-nut, which every one stepped forward and touched before they finally dispersed.

While I lingered round the canoe-sheds, the king came up to me, and asked me to come and see what he called his shed. This showed all the signs of having lately undergone a thorough repair. It appears that his brother had been lately killed in war with a tribe further to the westward, and therefore, out of respect to his memory, he had restored the whole building, and had carved a porpoise out of wood, life-size, inside of which he had placed his brother's bones. This fish was lying on supports in the middle of the shed, between two large canoes, the property of the deceased.

One could scarcely expect to find such respect for the dead, or such deep fraternal affection, in a man that stood before one, dressed only in a straw hat and a bracelet.

It is difficult to find what religion these islanders profess to have, if any. The shark seems to be their principal god. They told me that each village was supposed to have its own particular shark as a protecting deity; to it they make offerings of betel-nut and other things, when starting on a canoe voyage, believing that in case they are wrecked, this shark will see them safe to land. The taboo enters into some of their customs, for no woman is allowed to enter into their large canoe-sheds until some woman of another tribe has been killed, and her skull hung up as a trophy in the shed; nor is any woman allowed to get into their big war or fishing canoes, which can always be distinguished by their decorations of scarlet tassels.

The sun had now sunk behind the hills, and I rowed back to the vessel, a good many of the natives accompanying me. As night drew on a wonderful stillness reigned, only broken by the hooting of some night-bird. Later on some natives lit a large bonfire on the beach, and sitting round it, sang for some hours. Their music is wonderfully soft and low, sweet falsetto notes running up and down through a deep bass humming accompaniment. The night was so still and hot, that we all prepared to sleep on deck. The dark forms of the savages faded from view as the fire on the beach sunk lower, but every now and then they shone out lurid and fiend-like, when one of them would from time to time rise from his place and throw a dead palm branch on the smouldering embers. The branch crackled loudly as it burst into a flame, a shower of sparks rose into the air, and every neighbouring cocoa-palm stood out in fine relief against the dark background. The grim wooden figures in the canoe-shed, and the ghastly rows of skulls, shone out clearly for a few seconds, and then nothing more was to be seen, only the soft hymn-like music of the islanders went flowing on.

Long before daylight we were up, roused by the noisy chattering and fidgeting of countless parrots and other birds. I cannot call it singing, when I think of the sweeter notes of our English birds, still, it was very cheering and refreshing, and formed a strong contrast to the drowsy music of the previous evening.

First started our photographic party, and then I, mounted on an inverted tub on deck, with suitable articles of trade in a basket by my side, opened the market, and commenced the business of the day.

Never were there such good natives for trading, and to encourage them I bought everything.

Yams and cocoa-nuts were purchased for our future wants, and combs, armlets, necklaces, and their various weapons soon grew into a heap by my side. My rule was to refuse nothing, for then, the natives finding that nothing came amiss in this market, brought everything that they could think of, and in this way, amongst much rubbish, I secured things that I valued.

I found, however, that they had no pigs for sale. The king said he was sorry his tribe had none, but volunteered to accompany me in person to a town further to the west next day, where he assured me I should get plenty.

Accordingly we started early next morning, in my boat, manned by my South Sea Island crew. On our way we passed the mouth of a large cave, and paused for a few minutes to look at it—it was truly a wild and weird-looking place.

We were now outside of any sheltering reef, and therefore the waves of the unbroken ocean rushed into it with a hollow bellowing noise. Inside the cave was dark as pitch, and we rowed as near as the swell would admit. From out of the cave came shrill chattering and wild screams, and every now and then large vampire bats flapped about the entrance. The sounds we heard came from these creatures, that must have swarmed inside. In and out and about the mouth of the cave, fluttered and sailed a cloud of tiny swallows, looking far too pretty and airy-like for such a place; they are, I fancy, the cave swallow, that makes the edible bird's-nest so much prized in China. We waited some few minutes, rising and falling on the heavy swell outside this place, that reminded one of old John Bunyan's mouths of hell, and then rowed on to the westward.

On arriving at our destination, some four or five miles further on, I opened the market, and had the satisfaction of returning with a good load of likely-looking porkers. Here as at Makira I refused nothing that the natives brought me. The boys even brought me flowers and insects; amongst the latter were some large locusts and mantis, and a specimen of the "great shielded grasshopper," mentioned by Wallace as being found in New Guinea, of which too he gives a drawing. Here also I bought in abundance the eggs of the megapode, exactly similar to those I had seen at Niuafu, but I could not procure a live specimen of the bird itself.

The natives are very fond of tame parrots, I purchased a good many from them. Sometimes they will offer opossums for sale, and what at first appears a strange pet, the large vampire bat. This latter, however, makes a very interesting pet, and it would be difficult to find a more affectionate and faithful creature. From the existence of such animals it is evident that one now approaches the Australian fauna. Cockatoos do not exist in San Christoval, though the neighbouring islands of Guadalcanar and St. Isabel abound with them.

Here, too, are found alligators, but the natives assured me they are harmless, only sometimes carrying off a pig or a dog. I much regret that I did not bring away one of these dogs. They are horrid little curs, but often have a brush almost like a fox. The natives appear to value them for food, and for their teeth, out of which they manufacture necklaces.

On Friday, September 5th, we sailed out of Makira with the early land-breeze, a perfect fleet of small canoes accompanying us to the mouth of the harbour. The Makira lad whom I had brought from Rotumah had, as soon as I had anchored in the harbour, gone on shore to his friends, and I of course thought I had seen the last of him. To my surprise, however, the evening before we started, he came on board and begged me to let him go on with me. I had always found him a very useful and willing boy and at once consented.

One of the small canoes that paddled close to the side of the vessel, as we slowly moved out of the harbour, was occupied by a girl, sister of this boy. She seemed to be in great sorrow at his departure, her heart was apparently too full to speak, but her large anxious eyes followed every movement of her brother about the vessel. Here, thought I, is an instance of true sisterly devotion even in this degraded offspring of cannibals; here is an incident worthy of the pen of J. Fenimore Cooper or Captain Mayne Reid, and it pained me to think that in consenting to take this boy on with me, I was the cause of grief to his relations. He, heartless young scamp, took no notice of her, and positively turned his back on her. But she, paddling her canoe close up to where he leant against the bulwarks, fixed her sad eyes upon him. All at once an idea seemed to strike the boy, and coming up to me he asked for two sticks of tobacco; I gave them, and turning towards his sister he threw them into her canoe and walked away. She without a word or a gesture of thanks, but only with an expression of satisfied greed, hastily snatched up the tobacco and paddled straight back to the town, with all the air of a strange dog stealing a bone. Away flew all my dreams of sisterly devotion, and the romantic picture of a heart sorrowing under unrequited affection. The tobacco was all she wanted, she stuck to her brother till she had got all she could out of him, and went home, in all probability, only to regret that she had not managed to screw more out of him while she had the chance. The rest of the canoes still followed us some way out to sea, a strange and pleasing contrast to the timidity and suspicion they had shown on our arrival.

On September 6th, we were off the north-west point of San Christoval, and following the coast round we presently opened up a wide bay. In it I could see no houses or natives, but cocoa-nut trees in abundance; considering, therefore, that where there was so much food there would be inhabitants, I lowered the boat and was rowed towards shore. The beach was very rocky and it was some time before I could find a landing place; very soon some natives showed themselves on the beach, and ran down the shore keeping up with us as we slowly paddled on, looking for a soft place to land on. We found at last a strip of sand between some rocks, and running the boat in jumped out as quickly as we could to avoid being drenched in the surf; in a moment the natives had seized hold of the boat, and hauled it up high and dry out of the reach of the waves. This was all very well, but I could not help feeling that we were now very much in the power of the islanders. However, they proved very civil, and on my inquiring for pigs told me they would fetch some if I would wait. I fancy that any one who reads my travels will imagine that I went from island to island looking for provisions. The fact is, that amongst strange natives it is well to pretend that you have some object in visiting their town or they will suspect you are up to some mischief, such as kidnapping. In this case I consented to wait for the pigs, and leaving my boat in charge of the crew went for a walk round the bay. The jungle possessed its usual beauty, but on the ground there lay countless numbers of a species of centipede, some of them must have been at least eight or nine inches long; they appeared stupid animals, in a state of torpor, but they lay so thickly together that it was difficult to avoid treading on some of them. I have seen similar insects of a smaller size in Fiji, and there the natives told me that they could squirt out a poisonous juice which was dangerous if it happened to touch one's eye. There seemed no great probability of their doing this, but they have a very mischievous and snakelike appearance. I saw no signs of inhabitants, but about two miles down came on a fine stream, that did not enter the sea, or more properly did not flow into the sea above the surface. For the heavy surf had thrown up such a bar of sand and shingle, that the stream was dammed back and formed a fine clear lagoon. Here I was told a large town had once stood, but the people a few years ago had been vanquished in war and driven away by their enemies.

When I reached my boat again, I found the natives had brought no pigs, and had not even been to look for them, as far as I could judge. So in no very good humour I launched the boat and returned to the vessel, now at some distance in the offing. We continued sailing down the coast, and a few miles further down a large canoe was seen coming off to the vessel; we backed our topsail and waited for it. Now, too, the small "gulf islands," Ugi and Piu, were plainly visible ahead of us. The canoe was soon alongside, and the natives showing no distrust came on board at once. They had brought little or nothing for sale, but on my asking for pigs assured me that if I would go ashore to their town I should get plenty. In spite, therefore, of my disappointment at the last place, I had the boat lowered and went on shore, taking some trade with me and my guns to try and get some pigeons.

Arrived on shore, I walked about inspecting the town while the natives went to fetch their pigs, and I at the same time sent two of my boys to shoot pigeons; they returned in a very short time with about twenty. In the town I came on some most elaborately carved houses; the owner of the best one that I saw seemed very proud of his establishment, on the cross beams were carved fish and birds in high relief, and between these carvings were grotesque paintings, representing fishing parties in canoes, rainbows, waterspouts, &c. I confess I should hardly have guessed what some of the subjects were, had they not been explained to me. Many of the carved figures of birds and fish had been broken to all appearance quite recently, and in answer to my enquiries I was told it was because the son of the owner of the house had died, and he in a wild excess of grief had set to work to demolish that which must have taken years to complete. In this village I saw a young man, a native of the neighbouring island of Malanta. He had been brought over by a party of natives and sold as a slave. He was a tolerably good-looking lad, and would have been better if a large hole had not been bored right into the centre of the tip of his nose. Judging from this specimen of Malanta, I had good hopes that I might be able to open up communication with the people of his island, which I intended visiting next. I was not disappointed in my pig market here, for towards evening I bought a good supply and returned to the schooner. I decided to wait off this town all night, and in the morning send the photographic party on shore, for the carved houses seemed worthy of a picture.

I had endeavoured to explain to the natives what I wanted to buy, so the following morning the vessel was surrounded with canoes soon after daylight. I remained on board all day, but with the exception of some orange cowries got little that was different from the purchases made at Makira. Here, too, just as at almost every place I have visited, some of the natives wanted me to take them away in the vessel, not many, but perhaps half-a-dozen at a time; of course I refused, having no use for them. About noon the photographing party returned after a successful day, one man, the owner of a well carved house, was so civil that, finding the light in the interior was not sufficient to show the carvings, he without hesitation pulled down one whole side of his house; this I thought was civility rarely to be met with.

We now stood away for Malanta, passing on our way the low island of "Contrarieties," the native name for which is "Ulana," and at 6 A. M. were off the entrance to the harbour Malanta which has been called Port Adam.

A very strong current swept us in through the entrance, and as we rounded to inside, intending to anchor under a small island on the right hand, we were caught by an eddy, which nearly swept us on to the sandy beach. This was rather uncomfortable, for we saw many armed natives on the beach, and a quantity of large war canoes crowded with men lying off in the harbour watching us; however, we managed to back the vessel off with the assistance of our boat, and dropped anchor. Before entering the harbour I had prepared all my arms, and had shown each man his weapon and cartridges, so that in case of attack, every one could run at once and pick up his own gun or rifle. My opinion has always been that it is better amongst doubtful natives not to show any arms till it is absolutely necessary; it is well to be prepared to show them at a moment's notice, but never to produce them until it is evident that the natives have some treacherous or hostile intentions. Besides, a firearm in the hands of a nervous or excited man (for it is most exciting work when amongst doubtful natives) might be exhibited with too much ostentation, and this might give rise to a sudden alarm amongst the strangers, which would very probably end in hostility and bloodshed. All the weapons therefore were placed out of sight, but ready to be produced at a moment's notice.

For some time no canoes could be persuaded to come near the vessel, but at last one with two men in it came near enough to allow me to throw some pieces of tobacco into or near the canoe; then I made signs to them that I would buy their bows and arrows, and timidly and distrustfully they paddled near and handed up the articles in question, receiving pipes and tobacco in exchange. Seeing this, some other canoes came near, and as I stood on the deck gesticulating to them and throwing them small articles of trade, they began to gain courage and came close to the vessel. They were truly a wild and savage-looking lot, their rough, coarse, uncombed hair hanging over their shoulders; all were stark naked, but well armed with bows, arrows, and wicker shields; they had nothing with them but arms. They now gathered round the vessel in a most excited state, shouting and gesticulating to one another, and creating such a hubbub that I could hardly hear myself speak. From my elevated position I could now look into all their canoes, but I saw nothing in any of them but bows and arrows, nor could I discover a single article of trade such as cocoa-nuts or yams. Before me there was only a struggling, tossing mass of naked savages all well armed.

I decided therefore to endeavour to buy up all the arrows, and then perhaps they might produce something else, but their supply was inexhaustible, canoes went on shore and returned with nothing but arrows. I got one or two small pieces of tortoise-shell, and then I purchased the nose-rings from their noses, and the ear-rings from their ears, this with the exception of bracelets made of shell was all they wore—in fact, it was evident that no one considered himself decently dressed without them. All the while, however, the din grew louder and louder, and the arrows bristled thicker and thicker. By this time too crowds were hanging on to the vessel's sides and not a few had ventured on deck, but always with the same wild distrustful air.

And now, too, would come one of my crew and then another asking me to use caution, and saying that we were not safe, and begging me to prevent these savages from coming on deck; and while I was looking one way, a savage would reach out and steal some beads or a clay pipe, and run off with it; at which I did not like to look cross or even serious, for I was anxious by some means or other to give these people the idea that we were friendly, and only wanted to trade with them. In vain I searched the dusky throng to see if I could find any chief or king through whose influence I might check this awful hubbub. But my eye ranged in vain over this tossing, struggling, yelling crowd of naked humanity to discover that divinity which is said to hedge a king. Feeling, therefore, that all the responsibility rested with me, I yielded to the wishes of others, and decided to get up the anchor.

My boat was lying astern of the vessel, and the first thing was to get that up into the davits. This I knew would have to be done with great deliberation, and I therefore endeavoured, amid the general din, to make some of the natives understand that they must move their canoes out from the side of the vessel, in order to let the boat come alongside to be hoisted into the davits. I don't know how exactly to express what my feelings were at the moment, but I think I have felt something like it before, when going up to a strange horse in a stall with a handful of oats, for a fear always seizes me that he may mistake my excellent intentions, and meet my advances with a well-delivered kick.

I thought the natives seemed to understand what I wanted, and told my boys to pull the boat up slowly by its painter. Just what I feared took place. At the first sight of this movement on our part there was a yelling and screeching that deafened one; those in the canoes shouted to those on deck, and these latter, with a wild shout, leapt into the sea and swam to their canoes or towards the shore. Now then, I thought, for a flight of arrows, and I stood on deck waving to them, and smiling, and shouting all sorts of nonsense, but all the while prepared to duck down behind the cabin skylight at the first sight of a bow being drawn. They quieted down, however, when they saw us haul the boat up; and then we got up the anchor, the schooner swung round, and we steered out of the harbour by another passage further west.

I was very sorry to leave in this unsatisfactory manner. I had hoped to be able to push further west towards New Guinea, but I saw now that we could not hold our own amongst these people, and gave the order to steer for the Caroline group, where I knew we should find a more friendly people. On my return to New Zealand, I learnt that these Malanta natives had only a few weeks before my visit massacred a whole boat's crew of white men that had put in here after being shipwrecked. This would explain the wildness of the people, for they must have thought that I had come in to revenge the death of my countrymen.

CHAPTER VI.

AS we steered north for Ascension Island, we met with much calm weather. The sea, however, literally teemed with life. A bucket full of salt water poured into a large white basin was found to contain a marvellous collection of marine life. There were tiny jellyfish of the most perfect shapes and varied hues; and still more minute fish of a brilliant blue, not a quarter of an inch long. These latter were generally attendants on "Portuguese men-of-war," or were seen lurking under some small lump of jelly. Several specimens of blue shells were also taken floating on the surface of the water, generally attached to a slimy patch of foam, which appeared to act as a kind of float. In one of these patches I found quite a collection of minute brown shells. On the 16th, we crossed the equator, in 159° E. long.; and on the

17th, a curlew settled on the bulwarks of the schooner; we made several unsuccessful attempts to catch it. On the 19th and 20th we passed through immense quantities of driftwood. Huge trees and logs of wood were seen floating on all sides, looking as if they might have floated off from some suddenly submerged island. Whilst we were among this driftwood, we saw immense flocks of terns and boatswain birds. The water was alive with fish of all sizes. Large albacore splashed and jumped on all sides, evidently in pursuit of the smaller fish that hung round the large floating trees.

These were no doubt, in their turn, preying on the smaller creatures that lived on the timber. Above them all fluttered vast flocks of terns, incessantly darting down in pursuit of small fry. It struck me that in this marine settlement the albacore had certainly the best of it.

All the timber appeared to have been a long time in the water, for nearly all the logs were white with barnacles, and thoroughly honeycombed by the teredo. With a tackle I hauled one good-sized log on board. The fishy smell from it was most offensive. We split it up with an axe, and found it was thoroughly honeycombed and black to the heart; in doing this, we disturbed quite a small population; for in addition to multitudes of barnacles, we saw a variety of marine insects and a quantity of small crabs. The larger crabs had dropped off as we hauled the log on board. The fishy smell from this log was so overpowering, that it was a relief to every one when the examination was concluded, and the fragments committed to the deep.

Why should there be such a marvellous collection of driftwood here? It is a fact worthy of notice that when, heading south, we crossed these latitudes thirteen degrees further to the eastward, we passed through similar drifts of timber.

On the 19th, a heavy squall came down from the west, and just ahead of it flew a solitary wild duck, as if hurrying away from or driven onwards by bad weather. We must at the time have been at least 100 miles from land.

Just before sunset on the 20th, we sighted the high land of Bonabi or Ascension Island; and going under easy sail all night we found ourselves by daylight at the entrance to Roan Kiddi Harbour, on the south-west side of the island.

With the rising sun came violent and shifting squalls, with very thick weather, so that we did not dare to attempt this difficult entrance for some hours; but at last, with the sailing-master on the fore yard, we ventured in, and anchored in seven fathoms, nearly opposite the mouth of a river.

The water of the harbour was thick and muddy, and the whole shore fringed with mangrove swamps, that made landing impossible, except at the mouth of the river. The coral reef runs out a long distance from the island, and on it here and there are small, low, sandy islets, covered with cocoa-nut trees. Inside the reef at low water extensive mud flats are left quite dry, on which there are small patches of dwarf mangrove, endeavouring to establish themselves. Altogether, one misses the crisp freshness of scenery that surrounds the South Pacific islands. Mangrove swamps and mud flats are a poor exchange for the snow-white foam of the coral reef, and the bright emerald green of the water inside. Very few houses were visible from the vessel; only one on the summit of a hill that overlooked the mouth of the river, and a few huts on the small islets that lay off on the reef.

The anchor, however, was scarcely down before several canoes made their appearance. These looked clumsy and roughly put together, after the graceful little vessels of the Solomon Islanders. They all had outriggers, and were thickly coated with red paint.

The natives appear small and slight, somewhat darker than Polynesians, and have straight black hair. It was pleasant, too, to find that they were decent in their appearance, and did not indulge in the fantastic costumes of the Melanesians.

Almost all the occupants of these canoes spoke some English. I had no occasion here to try and open up communication by asking for pigs, for they were anxious to begin trading at once; but as it was Sunday, I of course refused, and told them to wait till to-morrow, when I would buy anything they brought. Then the poor wretches, accustomed only to the visits of American whalers, made offers that were sad to hear. The few natives who have adopted Christianity did not come off to the vessel; but I saw them standing in a group near the house that overlooked the mouth of this river, which I was told was the mission station. This was indeed a case of acting up to their religion, for they could not tell that I was not going to commence trading at once; and they must have thought that the heathen community would secure all the most coveted articles, and overstock my vessel with provisions before Monday morning.

At daylight on Monday I commenced trading—in fact, before daylight; and I was glad to see the Christians were among the first, they having during the night managed to dig up their taro and catch their fowls in time for this very early market. Prices, as the papers say, ruled high; there was a slight fall towards the middle of the day, but finally the market closed firm. What amused me most was the Americanism of these people; everything was valued by dollars and cents, although never at any time did money appear in the transaction. Thus, if a native said he wanted three dollars for his pig, I would say, "Very good;" and he would then say he wanted to take his money out in a knife, or some calico or tobacco; and I was quite at liberty to put a very extravagant price on all my trade. I must do the natives the justice to say that they were terribly afraid of being taken in, no doubt having had some bitter experiences in their dealings with Yankee skippers.

When I commenced buying from them, I was surprised to hear them asking ten or twenty dollars for a pig, thinking they expected me to hand that amount of money over; but I soon found nothing was further from their thoughts. So I only had to raise the price of my knives or tobacco to meet the standard of their market, and then business proceeded well enough.

Poor things, they think themselves very smart and Yankee-like, and "guess" and "calculate" continually. A pig of either sex is always known as a "hog;" and their miserable little apologies for domestic fowls, be they gouty old cocks, or hens long past laying, are here, as in the United States, described as "chicken." They always commence their sentences with "Say," and being a naturally good-tempered and obliging people, are always ready to "fix" anything for you.

I heard one story of the sharp practice of a Yankee skipper, that still remains undiscovered by the natives.

The chiefs are very fond of buying small boxes of

American tobacco, which hold, I think, about 30 lbs. These they never open, but store up in their houses, and, in fact, look on them much as we should on old and valuable china. The Yankee skipper having heard of this weakness of theirs, proceeded to turn it to good account. He brought a number of these small boxes in his vessel, and having carefully opened them, took out the tobacco, and put in a brick, carefully packing it so that it should not rattle about. These were traded away to the chiefs in exchange for tortoiseshell. Whilst here, I was shown by a resident white man a number of boxes in a native house which, I was assured, had all been treated in this way. I was very sorry for the unfortunate possessor, but did not feel it was my duty to undeceive him, or it might have gone hard with the white man living here, who, no doubt, would have been considered a participator in the fraud, and, for all I know, with good reason.

But after all, this possessor of empty tobacco boxes was no more taken in than the average number of English men and English women, who go into a shop and buy old china or antiques in general.

It appears that at this island it is considered a breach of etiquette not to call on the chief, who rejoices in the not very awe-inspiring title of "Nannikin." I was led to believe by the natives who came off to my vessel that if I wished to do the thing really nicely, I ought to go on shore at once, and pay my respects.

Had he been a wild savage I certainly should have done so; but I dreaded the idea of visiting a chieftain whose so-called civilization had been instilled into him by whalers. In the course of the first morning I received many hints from natives, who were evidently sent by his majesty to urge me to go and see him. And in addition to these hints, several times a man came up and asked me what I was going to give the Nannikin. I assured him that I intended to give the Nannikin positively nothing. This statement would be received with a blank stare of amazement, which gradually gave way to a smile of incredulity. I did not then properly understand that smile; but I do now. I afterwards found that the teasing old savage's powers of begging would have done credit to any charitable society. Late in the afternoon I rowed on shore to see this Nannikin. After proceeding up the river, which runs through mangrove swamps and dense bush, and occasionally passing a house which always seemed to me to have been built in the most unhealthy spot possible, I landed, and walked up a very muddy path, till I came to a small shed with no walls, under which I found the Nannikin seated, with one or two inferior chiefs squatting near him. In front of him were about a dozen natives, pounding up kava roots with heavy stones on a large, flat stone. This was at any rate a cleanlier process than that in vogue at Fiji or Rotumah, and other Polynesian islands, where the root is always chewed.

I shook hands with Nannikin, and sat down by him. He appeared to be a disagreeable and dissipated-looking savage, small and slightly-built, like all his subjects, but with a villainously foxy expression of countenance. I began a conversation with him, and asked him to come off to my vessel, and was getting on very well—in fact, I felt I was just beginning to get amusing—when in came a native with a basket of something. This stank so awfully, so overpoweringly, that I was obliged to subside. The very air felt heavy and oppressed with the horrible stench. Had his object been to put a stop to my talking, he could not have adopted a better method. I saw the stuff. In colour and consistency it exactly resembled that yellow grease that porters put on railway carriage wheels. They told me it was made of bread-fruit. I said good-bye, and hurried down to my boat.

It was a great relief to get out of the steamy atmosphere of the river bed into the open harbour. The water of the river, though clear and running swiftly over a pebbly bottom, is of a bright brown colour, and reminded me of the streams that flow from an Irish bog.

I found that the only resident missionary here is a native of Manilla, working under the American Missionary Society, that has its headquarters in Honolulu. He came off to me this evening, and sat a long time with me, speaking English well. He gave encouraging accounts of the spread of Christianity, saying that although, in this district, there are at present only sixty converts, yet that some gradually added themselves to his flock, and that in time he hoped all would join.

The Christians have all separated themselves

from the heathen, and now live in houses near the mission-house, on the left bank of the river. The missionary was the bearer of a present from his wife, consisting of a fan worked by herself, and a very pretty shell, giving me her "dear love, because I was a Christian." This was, I suppose, because I had refused to trade on Sunday.

In the morning I had sent off a Bonabi boy with my gun to get pigeons for me; he returned late in the evening with fifty. But he begged me to give him another time a weaker gun, for that one hurt his shoulder. I had provided him with an old pin-cartridge breech-loader, but he did not appreciate it, and asked for a muzzle-loader, with which I supplied him next day.

The pigeons are small, but very numerous; nor have I ever seen any bird so coated with fat. Their bodies were literally cased in fat, which had to be peeled off them before they were fit to be cooked. This fat proved very useful to us for oiling guns or anything that would be injured by rust. Vegetable oil in this climate is worse than nothing at all.

The following morning we rowed over to some of the small islets that lie out on the reef, and having hauled the boat up on shore, we went exploring about the reefs and shallows. Where the mud flats were covered with about six inches of water, we found it quite hot; the sea was, in fact, almost too hot for our bare feet. Finding in our walk a large rocky pool full of fish, we threw in a charge of dynamite, and secured a good basketful. We have found dynamite most useful in this part of the world. Tropical fish will very seldom take a bait, they appear to have enough to eat without it; but, besides this, their mouths, as a rule, are so small that our fish-hooks are not adapted for catching them, and it happens that when the fish are found to take the bait they are rarely caught, for, from the formation of their mouth, they are able, as it were, to suck off the bait as fast as it is offered to them.

Dynamite would, however, be of little use without a crew of South Sea Islanders ready to dive into the water directly after the explosion has taken place, for fish of any size sink at once to the bottom, only the small and useless ones rising to the surface. Whilst scrambling about the reefs and shallows, I saw many sharks, or, perhaps more properly, dog-fish, swimming in water too shallow to cover them. The huge ground-shark of Australia is known to have taken its prey in about two or three feet of water.

I found the small islets were not inhabited; there were houses on them, but these appear to be occupied only at certain times, for fishing parties, or perhaps at the season when the turtle come on shore to lay their eggs.

In this harbour I bought a good deal of excellent tortoiseshell, and an inferior kind of mother o' pearl. The reefs are literally covered with bêche-de-mer; they lie so thickly in the shallows that it is difficult to avoid treading on them.

The following day I received a visit from the Nannikin. He was dirty and disagreeable, and scarcely had set foot on the vessel's deck before he asked for something to drink. This was given him, and he at once proceeded to ask me what I was going to give him for coming into his harbour. Now considering that we lay off the harbour some hours before venturing to come in, there was ample time for some of the natives to have come off and assisted us in entering this most difficult passage; but none had appeared. So, in answer to his question, I told him that when he marked out the entrance to the harbour with buoys and beacons, and had a staff of pilots as we have in England, I should feel bound to pay him for entering the harbour.

Then he changed the subject, and sold me some tortoiseshell, and after that wanted more drink, and then went back to the old subject of a present, and his attendants chimed in, begging me to give the Nannikin something or he would never go away. So I felt that I was fairly saddled with this old man of the sea, and in sheer despair gave him some calico and tobacco; and then he sold me more tortoiseshell, and wanted more drink, which I refused him, and he went away.

Then I called to mind the smiles of those natives who had refused to believe that I would give the Nannikin "positively nothing;" and I felt that, in my ignorance, I had not properly gauged the old savage, or his powers of begging. I felt that I had been defeated; but it was a relief to get rid of this most unkingly king at any price, and I trusted that he would not repeat his visit, for all the time that I was being bothered by him there were natives waiting to sell me old shell and stone axes, and various articles that I particularly wished to secure.

Hearing that there were some remarkable mounds to be seen some few miles back in the hills, I determined to visit them; and as the state of the tide next morning would not admit of landing in my boat, I got into a small canoe with one native, and was paddled on shore. As usual, we landed at the mouth of the river, and the path we took was very swampy, and interlaced with the roots of the forest trees. These, owing to the damp climate and constant rain, were covered with a coat of slime, which made them as slippery as ice; and I suffered many a fall that day from treading carelessly on one of these roots, whilst watching some beautiful bird, or admiring some of the splendid vegetation. After leaving the houses surrounding the mission-house, we saw no natives or houses, and continued for about five miles staggering on through mud, across streams and over slippery roots, till we suddenly emerged in a clearing in the forest. I now remembered that I had noticed many such clearings on the hills as I approached the island in the schooner.

Certainly this open space had all the appearance of being cleared artificially. It was oblong, and contained about thirty acres, the soil being composed of a red gravel, in marked contrast to that which was seen in the forest, which was a rich black loam, capable of supporting any amount of vegetation. Here in the clearing nothing grew but tufts of wiry grass, ferns, and clumps of dwarfed mimosas. When we had got two-thirds of our way across this clearing, we came on these mounds. I found they consisted of one long earthwork, about twelve feet high, and twenty feet thick at the base; it commenced about 150 yards from the edge of the forest, and continued for a long distance into the forest, possibly for a quarter of a mile. It is not built in a straight line, but winds about a good deal, and had to me the appearance of being hurriedly and carelessly thrown up. I should imagine that it was put up before this clearing in the forest existed, or perhaps when the clearing was more extensive; for surely no one would build an earthwork in a dense jungle and extend it into an open clearing, or, on the contrary, commence it in a clearing and extend it into a forest. I sat long on this mound, and found from my guide that the natives had no tradition about this place, and after resting some time was obliged to leave it as wise as I came. Shortly after we commenced our return it began to rain heavily, and as at that moment we had reached a mountain stream, I stripped, and wrapping my clothes in the leaves of a gigantic arum, which were quite waterproof, I indulged in a bathe. The brook was beautifully clear but it swarmed with fresh-water prawns of large size; and these inquiring creatures seemed to find pleasure in standing on my feet, and then working all their legs and feelers; this tickled dreadfully, but at the slightest movement they darted off, only to return again with all the pertinacity of flies. In addition to this I saw gigantic brown eels curled round the large stones in the bed of the stream. Some of them must have weighed ten or fifteen pounds, and did not look at all pleasant neighbours. However I was careful not to disturb them, and as soon as the shower was over, had the satisfaction of finding my clothes were perfectly dry, and walked on home. Next morning I had a second wearisome visit from the Nannikin, who wanted me to buy his tortoiseshell; he was rude and importunate, and I was heartily glad when he left.

In the afternoon I rowed over to a small island where I was told a white man lived who had been there thirty years. Go to what island you will where the natives are at all friendly, in one of the first canoes that visits your vessel there will be a white man, or more properly the white man of the island. He and his class have been christened "beachcombers," for as they live on the shore, with no apparent means of support, they are supposed to exist on what the sea may throw up on the beach outside their door.

Your beachcomber has a style of dress which generally betrays to you that he was once a sailor. It is difficult to judge his age—you may guess anything from fifty to seventy. Dissipation and a tropical climate account for his withered appearance. He will generally be tatooed after the manner of the people with whom he has taken up his abode. He has sunk to the social and moral level of the natives, and has exceeded them in their vices. If he live amongst a kava-drinking people his eyes will be red and weak from an abuse of that preparation, and he will in all probability be suffering from hydrocele or elephantiasis. Give him a glass of grog and he becomes frank and friendly, probably in expectation of more. In fact, he only comes in the same spirit in which Gehazi followed Naaman; he has seen the vessel from his house, and has said to himself, "As the Lord liveth, I will paddle my canoe off to him, and take somewhat of him." In conversation with him you will quickly find that he has no code of morality and takes no trouble to conceal his lack. He is willing to make himself useful in any way during your stay as interpreter or general go-between 'twixt the ship's company and the natives. Are you purchasing a pig?—he pretends to be honestly working to get you a good bargain, while at the same time he is, in the spirit of the unjust steward, putting the natives up to demand exorbitant prices. And no doubt in this he acts with wisdom, for ships may come and ships may go, but he stays there for ever.

He discloses not his surname, but is known, and prefers to be known, only as Bill or Jack. Are you English?—he claims to be American; are you American?—he professes to be English. He has no property on the island, not even a pig or a fowl; he is too lazy to grow yams for his own use. Like the lilies of the field, he toils not neither does he spin, but is contented to be the humble retainer of the king or chief, and gets his food in his master's house. It is well, however, to be on good terms with the beachcomber, for if you want supplies, he, like Caliban, will "show thee the best springs, pluck thee berries, fish for thee, and get thee wood enough," or rather will see that this is done, for he does not care about work. Such is the genuine beachcomber, a variety of the genus *homo* now fast disappearing—a fact which is not to be regretted. For now a new style of white man is settling on the islands, trading legitimately with the natives. He will generally have a good house, though built in native fashion, and is as a rule a pretty decent man, eschewing sack and living cleanly, and is the agent or buyer of native produce for some Sydney or German firm in Samoa.

It is only just to say that the man I visited to-day was not a worthless beachcomber. His native wife I could not see, she having been bedridden for the last ten years; but I saw a number of his children, looking tidy and well cared-for. I found him busy at work constructing a windmill, which was to drive a machine for crushing the oil out of cocoa-nuts, or saw timber. He told me he had been some years at this solitary job, and I confess its completion looked to me as distant as that of Mr. Dick's Memorial. Here for the first time I tasted the durian—this must at present be its eastern limit. . A whaler had brought the seeds from the Philippines, and the trees grown from these seeds looked very flourishing and were loaded with fruit.

On the seaward shore of this islet there had been recently thrown up by the sea an enormous tree, foreign to the Caroline Islands. Those who understood, or pretended to understand, something about timber, said it was a Californian pine; it was full three feet in diameter, and sound to the very heart. The Nannikin on hearing of its arrival laid claim to it, and our friend on the islet had commenced squaring it previously to cutting it up for him.

If this pine actually came from the North American coast, one could scarcely expect it to arrive in such good condition. Lord Byron, of H. M. S. "Blonde," speaking of the Sandwich Islands, says that "it is remarkable that some of their canoes were built of pine wood, which does not grow in any of the islands. The trees are drifted thither apparently from the north-west coast of America. The great double canoe of Teraiopu was of two fine pine sticks that had been drifted to the islands." (See "Voyage of the 'Blonde' to the Sandwich Islands.")

Next morning at daylight we got under way, taking a native pilot with us to point out the entrance to Metalanien Harbour, on the eastward side of the island, where we proposed anchoring. I was glad to get to sea if only for a few hours, for natives, like unchecked children, have the art of teasing to perfection.

At 5 P.M. we anchored in the perfectly land-locked harbour of Metalanien. The anchor was hardly down before crowds of natives came off in their canoes, anxious to begin trading in the morning; but as it would be Sunday I refused. Next day we went in the boat to visit the marvellous stone ruins that are found here.

The entrance to Metalanien Harbour is merely a break in the coral reef, caused, I should imagine, by the flood of fresh water sent down by the river; and although there is a wide expanse of water inside, the deep channel leading to the anchorage is very narrow. To the left, on entering, shallow water extends for a mile or more, much of which is dry, or nearly so, at low water. In our trip to-day to the ruins which lie to the south of the harbour, we soon found our boat aground, and had to get out and wade, towing the boat after us, which was much impeded by the dense growth of seaweed. About two miles from the vessel, as we advanced, still towing the boat, we passed to our left, lying out in the middle of the mud-flats, a small wooded islet, about fifty yards in diameter. This had been artificially connected by a stone causeway with what we then thought was the mainland, but which we afterwards found to be a number of small islets, separated by narrow salt-water creeks. This causeway was about a quarter of a mile long, and may at one time have been well built, but at the present time it consists only of a row of large boulders, looking like gigantic stepping-stones. Near where the causeway joined the land, we turned up a narrow creek, which was walled on either side to the height of three feet, by basaltic prisms, built as people would now build what is known as a log and chock fence. The land here is very low, and there was a great deal of mangrove swamp. Two hundred yards up the creek we turned a sharp corner, the main channel here dividing itself into a number of smaller ones. And here, on the left bank of the extreme left channel, stood an angle of a lofty wall, about thirty-five feet high, overlooking the creek. This wall was entirely built of basaltic prisms, and followed in one direction the edge of the creek, up which we waded, while in the other it ran back into the dense mangrove swamp. The water was now so shallow that we had to leave the boat, and, wading up the creek, we came to a gateway, opening out into the creek, and passing this, we waded on till we came to the other end of the ruins, which also terminated in a lofty angle of a wall. The whole front of the building is about 100 yards in length. We now returned to the gateway, which appeared to be the only way of entering the building. The sill is raised about four feet above the creek, and is made of enormous basaltic columns laid flat. Stepping on these columns, we found ourselves in a large court, enclosed by walls rising to the height of about thirty feet. Round the whole court, built up against the inside of the outer walls, ran a terrace, eight feet high and twelve feet in breadth. This was built also of basaltic prisms. The whole of the court was not visible at once, for the dense vegetation entirely concealed what may be called the back part of the ruins, and it was only by clambering about, and pushing our way through vines and creepers, that we ascertained it was nearly square. The gate we entered at faced about north. This large court is divided into three courts by what are now low walls, running north and south, the gateway being in the centre of the middle court. In the middle of each of these three courts stands a chamber fourteen feet square, not excavated, but built of large basaltic prisms laid horizontally. There is no entrance to these chambers, but I managed to squeeze myself in between two of the columns in the roof of the centre one. I could not get into the other two chambers, but could see into them by looking through the spaces between the stones. The floor of each was covered with rubbish, which looked as if it must have been thrown in carelessly from time to time. Through both terrace and wall on the western side of the main court we saw several square openings level with the ground; stooping down and looking through, we saw they communicated with a muddy creek outside. With the exception of these openings, there is no entrance to the building, but by the gateway we entered at.

The outside walls, including the terrace, are quite twenty feet thick; and some of the stones, especially those in the front wall near the gateway, are of immense size. I measured some that were twenty-five feet long and eight feet in circumference.

Passing out at the gateway once more, and wading up the creek, we found that it, as well as the other branches, was walled up on either side to the height of three or four feet. Nowhere in the whole ruin could I see a trace of any instrument being used to shape any of the stones. The upper tier of stones on the outer walls of the court overhangs considerably, as if for defence.

In wading about I cut my foot, and was unable to visit the ruins, which are situated about a mile further westward on the sea shore, part of which we had seen as we sailed down the coast on Saturday. Some of our party went on, and described what they saw as an angle of a wall, built, not of basaltic prisms, but of enormous boulders, against which the sea dashed, and at the back of this was an inner and more elevated wall.

They declared that some of the stones must have weighed several tons. These ruins are of entirely a different description, no basaltic columns appearing in their construction, only vast unhewn rocks have been piled up so as to make what is now a very effective sea wall.

But it is very evident that the level of the land has altered much since these walls were built, for there are massive ruins standing out in the sea some distance from land, built of a similar and equally massive material.

While the rest of my party were absent, I sat down in the middle of those ruins we had first visited with my native guide. After some minutes' silence he asked me what I thought of these ruins, who made them, and for what purpose? I asked him in return if his people had no traditions connected with this place. He replied that they had none, but that they called them "Nan towass." I could get no translation of this name from him. I asked him if similar stones to these basaltic columns were found in other parts of the island, or if he knew where they were brought from. He answered, No, and gave me to understand that he had always thought they had been worked artificially into their present shape. I may here mention that Joseph Keogh, a white man who has resided on the island some years, told me that quarries of this stone existed on the north-west side of the island, that he had visited them himself, and that the columns lay horizontally in the bed, and were so loose that they could easily be picked out one by one. This spot, he said, was about twenty miles distant from the ruins.

A deep mystery hangs over the origin of these ruins. The opinion has been held by previous visitors that they are the work of Spanish buccaneers.

But this opinion I cannot hold. The fact of a Spanish brass gun having been found on the island, and a silver crucifix in the ruins, does not allow me to believe that the Spaniards were the builders. The ruins are so extensive and massive, such enormous stones have been used in their construction, that I imagine a very large population must have lived here at one time. And it seems preposterous that a few Spanish buccaneers should have gone to such a vast amount of labour to protect themselves against a race of savages armed only with slings and bows and arrows. Surely, too, Spaniards would have chosen a more commanding position, and would never have erected these fortifications on a low swampy group of islets hardly separated from the mainland. Would they not also have used some kind of mortar or cement?—for the neighbouring coral reef would have supplied them with abundance of lime for this purpose. Surely, too, the walls would have been loopholed for musketry. Are we to believe that the arrival of the present race on Bonabi is so recent as to be since the arrival and departure of the Spaniards, who are said to have built these ruins? for they know nothing of their origin. The residence of a strange people amongst them, powerful and numerous enough to have executed these works, would never have passed away from the minds of the natives.

I believe these ruins to be the work of a people that have passed away. Possibly Spaniards may have come, and for a short time occupied these ruins, an event which might have passed away from the recollection of the natives, just as Tasman's visit to New Zealand in 1642 was quite forgotten by the Maories in Cook's time, only 127 years after. A passing visit of the Spaniards would explain the existence of the silver crucifix found in the ruins. There is one thing which might be noticed in favour of its having been built by ancestors of the present race of natives, and that is, that the terrace all round the inside of the court is similar to the raised staging which runs round the modern huts of the natives, on which they sleep, and indeed live night and day, the centre part of the building being occupied by canoes, fishing apparatus, &c. Now, in a climate like that of Bonabi, where it rains every day, these ruins, if inhabited, must have required a roof, but they are too large to have been spanned by a single roof; possibly, therefore, the stone terrace which runs round the court may have been covered like the pent-house of a tennis court, and on it the people may have ate and slept, while the canoes were drawn up into the court-yard through those holes which I mentioned existed at intervals in the base of the outer wall. It is true that only small canoes with an outrigger could have been drawn up, but may we not consider the outrigger an invention that the Polynesians brought with them wherever they went?

The chambers in the centre of the courts I cannot

account for, though something similar is described as existing in some of the ancient temples of the Sandwich Islands.

A thorough excavation might throw more light on this subject, but I found the natives very unwilling to allow even a branch of a tree to be cut down, although of no value whatever. Consequently, our photographs do not give as clear a view of the ruins as would have been the case had we been allowed to make a considerable clearing.

Next morning the natives commenced trading with me, as usual, at daylight. This is a very good plan, for towards noon the sun is so powerful, that even under an awning it is scarcely possible to stand on deck, much less endure the noise and vexation that accompanies purchasing even the smallest article from a South Sea Islander.

Our photographic party started very early in the morning for the ruins; but, owing to the climate, not much was done in any one day. It rains here every day, and between the showers, or rather during the small intervals of fine weather with which we are blessed, the sun comes out with scorching heat, and the whole atmosphere is like a vapour bath.

It took therefore several days to get all the views that were wanted of these ruins.

The second day I lay here I received a visit from the king. I found him, like Nannikin, a degraded old villain. He too begged for presents, and expressed surprise and disgust at our not falling into the ways of the ordinary visitors to this harbour.

Every morning I used to go on shore at sunrise and get a fresh-water bath—no slight blessing in such a climate. The water was clear and cool, running fresh from the mountains, but here, as at Roankiddi, I found the prawns most irritating, and the eels a constant source of alarm. The natives were more afraid of them than I was, and, either from superstition or from a natural dislike to their appearance, which I have noticed in the Polynesians further south, refused to molest them in any way.

However, I had my revenge on the prawns; the boys used to catch abundance for me, which I was only too glad to purchase from them, for they were excellent. Here, too, I always got a superabundance of pigeons. I always sent two guns on shore every day, and on one occasion received a hundred and thirty birds as the result of a day's shooting. On

Thursday we sailed out of the harbour and bore away for the island of Oualan.

I never visited an island where were so plainly marked the evil effects of the inhabitants having been educated in crime by a villainous caste of whites. Naturally of a mild and easily-moulded character, they have taken the impression of the vagabond English, American, or Portuguese sailors that have been thrown amongst them. They have even been afflicted by the residence of runaway convicts, who here found a retreat where they could safely gratify their worst passions.

I had several requests from both natives and foreigners residing here to ship them in my vessel, especially as a Honolulu whaler was lying on the north side of the island too leaky to go to sea. The crew had been discharged, and all were living on shore. The conduct of the captain of this vessel was so bad that it shocked even the not over-sensitive white residents. One of the latter said to me, "They would hang him for it at home." It is indeed to me a marvel that missionaries should have done as much as they have amongst these people.

While people in England and America are generously supporting missionary societies, it is a pity that the strong counter-current of vice that is brought to bear upon the natives cannot be checked, and I wish it were possible to establish a society for the suppression and chastizing of these vagabond whites, to show them that now-a-days, even in this remote corner of the world, they cannot be allowed to carry on their abominably selfish conduct with impunity.

On the 5th of October we sighted on our lee bow the small low islands known as Macaskill's Islands, so we kept away a little to have a nearer view of them. They are very small and well wooded, and entirely surrounded by a coral reef.

Though I saw several large houses, resembling those at Bonabi, no natives showed themselves. The wind was light and baffling, and a very strong easterly current was experienced on the north side of the island, and as night was now setting in and no canoes came off to us, we stood away once more for Oualan.

CHAPTER VII.

T noon on Tuesday, Oct. 7th, we saw Oualan, thirty miles away to the south-east. At this distance it looked like two islands, for we had not yet raised the low land which runs in a strip right across the island, dividing the mountains in a most remarkable manner.

As we approached the land the wind headed us, and we had to beat round the north end of the island. By daylight next morning we found ourselves about eight miles to the north of Port Lélé. With the rising sun came as usual a very violent squall, and we had to let go sail after sail. When this passed off we were becalmed for some hours, but at noon a light air enabled us to stand in, and at 3 P.M. a boat came off with the king's son, who acts as pilot, and with him an old white man.

With the aid of their boat and our own towing us, we managed to get into the harbour, though it was quite dark, and anchored about 7 P.M.

In the morning we found we were lying about a hundred yards from the shore, on which stood the king's house and a few others. Soon after daylight I received a large basket of fish from his majesty, and a quantity of bread-fruit and taro ready cooked. In return for this I found he expected a jug of coffee and some bread and butter.

This interchange of civilities took place every morning of our stay here.

The morning after our arrival the rain came down in floods and I was not able to get on shore till eleven o'clock. I first called on the king who had given us such a hospitable reception, and found him living in a most excellent house, furnished with a sofa and chairs, kerosene lamps, &c.

He was dressed in European, or rather in American clothes, for he had on a very long "claw-hammer" coat, which would have gladdened the heart of a "down-easter." He was, however, a sad cripple from rheumatism, and I promised to send for my electric machine and give him some relief. His daughter sitting in another part of the house busy at her loom, made quite a picture; altogether I think I never saw such an air of respectability about a native family before.

I now went out to see the stone ruins that are found here. They are less extensive, but altogether similar in construction to those at Bonabi. I saw one high angle of a wall built of basaltic prisms, but with this exception the remains are not nearly in such a good state of preservation as those at Bonabi.

Mingled with the ancient ruins, there is a good deal of modern stone-work, the swampy paths are in places paved with slabs of stone, and the small plantations of the natives are all well secured by substantial stone walls; sometimes we walked on raised stone causeways, all this showing that the present race have a tendency to make use of stone. The low land we were on is only a small island lying in the harbour, and it is worthy of remark that these basaltic ruins are, both at Bonabi and Oualan, not on the mainland, but on low-lying islands hardly separated from the mainland, but inside the main coral reef. On the other side of the island we found a well-built modern sea-wall extending along the whole beach; it is evident that the sea is encroaching, and that the people are endeavouring to check it.

At spring tides a good deal of this part of the island is flooded by the sea, which leaves everywhere a débris of coral and small shells. At the western end of the island we came to the missionary's house and church, now unoccupied, and all about them the natives had built stone causeways raised three or four feet from the ground, affording excellent dry paths in all weathers.

If these people are not the descendants of the race that erected the ponderous ruins in the centre of this islet, they certainly have developed a great talent for using stone, for other natives would use only wood, or more probably do nothing at all to resist the encroachments of the sea.

We made the circuit of the island and returned to the king's house, when I gave him a taste of electricity, which he said relieved him much. I therefore left the electric machine at his house, having instructed him how to make use of it.

In the afternoon I had a visit from a German

living on the island, who brought with him some specimens of minerals, which he believed were silver. I am no mineralogist, but if they were not silver I don't know what they could have been. He would not, however, allow me to have a specimen, nor would he divulge the spot whence he got them. It is perhaps worth mention that the old Spanish navigators had an idea that silver was to be found in some of the South Sea Islands. Quiros, in an address to Philip II. of Spain, says: "It is to be observed, that in the Bay of St. Philip and St. Jago were found in one house many stones black and heavy, and that by chance they brought me two pieces, each as big as a nut, and that in the city of Mexico, one Don Francisco Bachoco, proprietor of mines, and one Diego Gomez de Molina, saw them in my lodging, and the one of them they showed me full of eyes of silver, and for this reason we carried it immediately to the house of an assayer, who put it in a crucible, and for his reasons gave it so much fire that the crucible broke, and thus nothing was seen; yet the other part remaining with me the assayer melted it again, and in it was seen a small point which expanded under the hammer.

"He presently touched it on three stones, and six silversmiths said it was silver touch; and for greater certainty they touched lead and tin and other known silver close to it, though there were some who said that the assay should have been made with quicksilver, and others with saltpetre and certain things. And the assayer affirmed that the metal was good, and here he touched the small point, and two silversmiths said that it was silver." So much for Quiros, but unfortunately he is the man who made the statement of their having built a town in the Bay of St. Philip and St. Jago in the New Hebrides, and of their having appointed officers to manage the city. In a note at the bottom of a page in a French translation of Quiros' voyages, I find the following:—" Les fonctions de ses officiers n'ont pas été de longue durée, non plus que la ville même où ils les exerçaient. Ceci peut bien passer pour une rodomontade espagnole."

Terrible liars were some of these old navigators, or perhaps they allowed other people to lie for them. Take for instance the cruise of Roggewein, a Dutchman, in 1722. He discovered Easter Island, and gives an interesting account of it. But in Dalrymple's collection of voyages there is an extract from the Dutch relation of Roggewein's voyage.

Here it is stated that when Roggewein was on the point of anchoring at Easter Island, " there came off to them a boat managed by a single man, a giant of twelve feet high, who exerted all his strength to escape us but in vain, for he was surrounded and taken." The writer then goes on with a description of the Dutchmen landing, which smacks more of the Odyssey than anything else :—

" On the 10th of April we made for the island in our boats, well armed in order to take a view of this country, where an innumerable multitude of savages stood on the seaside to guard the shore and obstruct our landing; they threatened us mightily with gestures, and showed an inclination to await us and turn us out of their country, but as soon as we, through necessity, gave them a discharge of our muskets, and here and there brought one of them to the ground, they lost their courage. They made the most surprising motions and gestures in the world, and viewed their fallen companions with the utmost astonishment, wondering at the wounds which the bullets had made in their bodies, whereupon they hastily fled, with a dreadful howling, dragging their dead bodies along with them.

"So the shore was cleared and we landed in safety. Thus far my narrative will gain credit, because it contains nothing uncommon. Yet I must declare that all these savages are of more than a gigantic size, for the men being twice as tall as the largest of our people, they measured one with another the height of twelve feet. So that we could easily—who will not wonder at it?—without stooping have passed between the legs of these sons of Goliath. But none of their wives come up to the height of the men, being commonly not above ten or eleven feet. The men had their bodies painted with a red or dark brown, and the women with a scarlet colour.

"I doubt not that most people who read this voyage will give no credit to what I relate, and that this account of the height of these giants will probably pass for a mere fable or fiction, but this I declare, that I have put down nothing but the real truth, and that this people, upon the nicest inspection, were in fact of such a surpassing height as I have here described." All this is very strange, but it is still stranger that when Captain Cook visited this island some years after, he found that the natives had assumed the average size of the human race.

On the 10th of October, accompanied by the German, I went to visit a large cave, which he said existed on the north side of the island. We had no occasion to go outside the reef that surrounds the island, but rowed inside through narrow muddy creeks that wound about in dense mangrove swamps. We had to leave the boat in the middle of one of these dreary places, and walk till we came out on a fine sandy beach on the north side of the island, and then following the coast westward for about a mile we turned into the bush, and about 500 yards back from the shore found ourselves under a high bold bluff into which the cave penetrates. The entrance was full fifty feet high, but dark and gloomy, overshadowed as it is with dense vegetation.

There was a most overpowering smell of ammonia inside, that almost made our eyes water; and we disturbed hundreds of tiny cave swallows and bats that fluttered about the mouth as long as we stayed. A few yards from the entrance we were stopped by a lake of peaty mud, which quite forbade any hope of advancing. We tried by laying bushes on the surface to advance over the mud, but found it was impossible, and the idea of being smothered in this awful quagmire deterred us from running any risk. It appeared to be deep, for we could not reach the bottom with long poles, even a short distance from the edge. So I burnt a blue light, which showed us all that was to be seen, and very much annoyed the bats and swallows, and then returned to the shore.

The low state of the tide would not admit of our returning to the vessel; so I took a walk out to the coral reef, picking up shells, and then, with four of my boys, went to a fresh-water creek, intending to have a bathe. The whole neighbourhood of the stream was burrowed like a rabbit warren, the work of a colony of large land crabs; and now my crew commenced a systematic hunt for them, for they assured me they were excellent eating. The boys boldly thrust their arms into the holes up to the shoulder, feeling for these crabs. I cannot understand how they escaped being bitten, but they never were, and from almost every hole dragged out a crab, strongly resisting; holding him in one hand, they broke off a vine that was always found growing within reach, and tied the animal up like the Davenport Brothers, when they would proceed to another hole and repeat the operation; and in a short time each boy had a number of crabs, tied and secured like a string of onions.

Tired of catching crabs, we adjourned to the stream for a bathe; but here all desire for bathing vanished, for we found that it swarmed with enormous eels. These are never molested by the inhabitants, but my boys rose superior to the superstitions of the natives. They sharpened some stout sticks, and, wading into the water, commenced to spear the eels. They were in every case so large that it required two of the boys to secure them when speared, and bring them to the bank. I never saw such monsters, some of them weighed at the least 25 lbs., and it was as much as two men could do to carry our load of eels down to the boat. I never eat eels, but these, from their brown colour looked especially forbidding, they wanted the silvery gloss of an English eel, which would almost persuade one that it was a fish.

We got back to the vessel about 5 P.M.

On Sunday, October 12th, I had a quiet morning

on board, and was glad to see that the natives, though deserted by their missionary, recognized the day. In the afternoon I rowed to the west side of the harbour, and, proceeding up a creek, had a pleasant bathe, and then walked on for a mile or so. I was now on the low land that seems to split the island into halves. It is a magnificent valley, and nothing can exceed the richness of the soil. It is several miles wide, and extends from one side of the island to the other, intersected by clear, running streams. Here would be a magnificent spot for an enterprising Englishman to settle. The climate is too damp for the growth of cotton, but I should imagine nothing could be better for sugar. And the land could be had from the natives at a very moderate figure, for they make no use of it whatever. The scenery, too, was very pretty, the fantastic peaks on the southern side rising almost abruptly from the plain.

Next day the king came on board, wishing to sell me some pigs and other provisions. I bought all that he had, though I found that royal pigs and royal taro were expected to fetch a very high price. I wished him good-bye when he had concluded his business, and aided by a light favourable breeze, sailed out of the harbour. I trust that here, as I have wished to do at each island, we left a good impression behind us. The king said he wished more ships like mine would come there, showing that he can appreciate a higher tone of conduct than that practised by whalers or riff-raff South Sea Island traders.

Oualan cannot but strike one with melancholy. Here are the last relics of a fine race of people, utterly ruined by their contact with whites.

The natives are more robust-looking than those of Bonabi, but they will soon be extinct. There are now not two hundred on this large and fertile island that used to hold its thousands. In the twelve months ending in December, 1872, upwards of sixty died, and already this year twenty-six have succumbed.

I found on shore here about twenty natives of Ocean Island : their country had been stricken with a famine, and some trading vessel had carried them on here out of kindness. They now wanted me to take them home again; but I declined, out of respect to the laws of my country. It is a pity they should be left here—heathens amidst a Christian community; and it is high time the American missionary returned to his post.

In addition to these there were three white men living in one house, with a large suite of half-castes of both sexes. They told me they had recently arrived from Pleasant Island. They had lighted on the place like a pestilence; and now, finding there was not much that suited them at this island, they were anxious to leave again, and begged me to take them to an island called Providence, which I found, on looking at the chart, lay considerably to the north. It appears there are only sixty to seventy natives there; and they gave me the paucity of the natives as one reason why they wished to be taken there. This I refused to do point blank; for with their retinue of about twenty Pleasant Island natives and half-castes of both sexes, they would soon have crushed, demoralized, and possibly enslaved a miserable population of sixty.

To carry them to any island would have been to convey a plague to the unfortunate inhabitants; and it would be far better that they should drink themselves to death where they are, before a vessel is found to assist them in their project. They appeared to have abundance of money, for they offered me 500 dollars to convey them. How they have come by it I know not. But Pleasant Island, from which they came, has about the worst name of any of the Pacific islands, owing to the presence of runaway convicts.

Such men as these, capable of lending themselves to any villainy, should be wiped off the face of the earth. When they told me they came from Pleasant Island, I took down a book from my shelf, and read them the following extracts from the log of a vessel that visited that island: "This island is infested by Europeans, who are either runaway convicts, expirees, or deserters from whalers, and are for the most part men of the worst description. They live in a manner easily to be imagined from men of this class—without either law, religion, or education to control them, with an unlimited quantity of ardent spirits which they obtain from distilling the toddy that exudes from the cocoa-nut tree. When under the influence of intoxication, the most atrocious crimes are committed by these miscreants. These fiends frequently urge the different tribes to warrant deeds of blood, in order to participate in the spoils of the vanquished. They are in constant dread of each other, and by their deeds even horrify the untutored savage."

The extract I quoted went on to say that on one occasion eleven Europeans were deliberately murdered by a monster named Jones. "He invited them all to a feast, and when he had got his victims intoxicated with the island spirit, he gave them food in which he had previously mixed poison. This proved fatal to seven. The remaining four having refused to eat, he watched his opportunity and shot them. Vain and futile will be the attempt to introduce Christianity and civilization, while these miscreants are permitted to remain with the natives, corrupting them by their baneful example and selfish advice, introducing intoxication and disease in its many horrible forms, and teaching these naturally mild and tractable men the grossest depravity."

Both at Oualan and Bonabi I collected all the old implements of the natives that were of ethnological interest, but naturally, amongst a people that have so long mixed with white men, they are scarce. At

Bonabi and Oualan I found sashes of banana fibre dyed of different colours, and skilfully woven on a loom. The patterns in many are very pretty, and I cannot but think they were introduced by the Jesuit fathers who started from Manilla for the Carolines, but were never afterwards heard of.

In Bonabi they have a peculiar kind of mat for sleeping on made of pandanus, quite different from any South Sea Island mat. This they call "lordge." Their pretty coronets of beads they called "tor," and their sashes or belts "maré."

Shell axes made from the tridacna were to be had in plenty, though never used now; some of these at Oualan were more than a foot in length. The shells from which it was cut must have been of enormous size. These they called "tolla." Stone pounders for beating up bread-fruit or taro they called "toxiak;" and sashes, similar in shape, but marked with a different pattern from those at Bonabi, they called "tall." The loom on which they are woven is known as "pyush."

But I procured many other articles both of use and ornament, though these latter are never worn at the present day.

We had a tedious time of it after leaving Oualan, meeting with calms and violent squalls, which latter necessitated our keeping a very careful watch, and we seemed to be perpetually letting go and pulling up the haulyards. On Monday, October 20th, we sighted Namarik or Baring's Island. It consisted of two small low islands with a lagoon enclosed by one coral reef. There is no passage through the reef, so we sailed up to the south-west side of the islands, and as no canoes came off to us, stood close in, and then saw a German flag hoisted on shore. The boat was immediately lowered, and I rowed towards this signal. As I neared the reef, a number of natives waded out through the shallow water, and pointed out to me the best place for effecting a landing. There was very little surf, and as soon as my boat grounded, a crowd of natives seized hold of her and pulled her up high on the smooth coral rock. I then walked on to the beach, where I was met by a German, who told me he lived on the island as agent for a German firm in Samoa, and was engaged in buying dried cocoa-nuts from the natives. This system of buying the dried nut from the islanders was first introduced by the Germans, and has now almost entirely superseded the system of buying the oil from the natives direct, which was always manufactured by them in a very tedious and awkward manner.

The German led me to his home, which stood near the beach hard by. He had a nice clean house, built of native materials, but separated into rooms, in which of course he had pictures of his Emperor and Bismarck. Round the house he had a really neat little garden, which is a luxury that ninety-nine Englishmen out of a hundred would never take the trouble to secure, were they placed in a similar position. As a rule, a white man living in the South Sea Islands lacks the cleanliness and small amount of order that the natives observe. In course of conversation, I found that my schooner had been taken for a Fiji kidnapper, and I learnt that it was by the German's advice that none of the natives had launched their canoes to come off to the vessel.

The people appeared very civilized, and in type of features more resembled the Kingsmill than the Caroline Islanders. They all had straw hats, and were decently covered by thick fringes of grass round the loins. On my informing them that I wanted to trade with them, they promised to bring off some provisions if the German would come off with them, for they were still very much inclined to be distrustful, and not one ventured to come off to the vessel till they saw the German actually in my boat, and fairly on his way to the schooner. We continued standing on and off the land, while canoes kept plying between the ship and the shore, bringing fowls and ducks and cocoa-nuts. I soon exhausted their limited supply, and at 3 P.M. landed the German and bore away for Bonham Islands.

We were now fairly in the archipelago of islands known as the Ralick Chain. And here we found our charts of very little use. The whole of the archipelago consists of groups of islands scarcely rising above the level of the sea, and enclosing a lagoon into which there is not always a passage for a vessel. We sighted Bonham Islands next day, and stood close in to try and find a passage. The islands appeared to be strung together like beads, and we looked in vain for a break in the reef, although I know that there are several ship passages into the lagoon. Thus we continued sailing down southwards, following the direction of the chain of islets. We saw no natives, nor any canoes, till we arrived at the south-west corner of the chain. Here a canoe sailed off to us, with five or six natives. We tried to persuade them to act as pilot for us, but they were so shy and distrustful that we could do nothing with them. Only one ventured on board with some cocoa-nuts for sale, and this he did so hurriedly, and with such evident fear of being kidnapped, that as soon as he had received a piece of tobacco, he took a flying leap over the side of the vessel and swam to his canoe, when they instantly bore away for land. This canoe was a very smart little vessel, and decidedly the most serviceable seagoing canoe I have ever seen. A number of shrouds supported the mast on the opposite side from the outrigger, and both stem and stern rose considerably, but scarcely more than in some of the Norwegian boats. Failing to find a passage, and night coming on, with anything but settled weather, we bore away for Mulgrave Islands. I was much disappointed not to be able to visit this group properly, but the charts of this part of the Pacific are so incorrect, that they are of little assistance, and these chains of islands are so very extensive, often fifty or sixty miles long, and one islet so exactly like another, that I could not spare the time to look for an anchorage.

The natives, in addition to this, though very civilized, have, on account of the Fiji labour traffic, learnt to look on all stranger vessels with distrust, and cannot be persuaded to come off.

We now experienced a succession of the most villainous weather. Violent squalls of wind and rain fell upon us night and day, at intervals of an hour or so; and we were perpetually kept on the move, taking in and setting sail. On the 25th, we sighted Mulgrave Islands,—it proved to be the north-west end of this very extensive group. The islands were without any distinguishing feature, being, like Bonham Islands, a chain of low, sandy islets, connected by a reef, and scarcely rising above the water. All night, under easy sail, we followed the coast-line, and next morning were becalmed about four miles from the land. I was determined to try and open up communications with this people, so rowed in my boat towards land. We had much trouble to find a landing-place, for a heavy surf appeared to break everywhere; but at last, taking advantage of a point of sheltering rocks, we ran the boat in, and landed, a crowd of natives at the same moment coming down to meet us. An old man, with his hair tied up in a knot on the top of his head, and thickly tattooed from his shoulders to his waist, made signs to us to follow him up into the bush. We therefore went after him, a crowd of natives and quite a pack of curs accompanying us. Our walk led us through swampy soil, sometimes spongy and peaty, and the island had the appearance of being gradually changed into a mangrove swamp. We passed several pools of water, but all, with one exception, contained only brackish water.

In a short time, we had crossed the island, and came out on the lagoon which this group of islands encloses. The water was smooth as glass, and of a most magnificent blue. Here were several houses; and I now found that all the inhabitants live on the inside of the chain of islands, and prefer to build their houses facing the lagoon, on the banks of which they keep all their canoes. The houses were very poorly built, but our guide led us into one, which proved to be the king's. His majesty, a man of about forty years, was lying down, and looking very ill. I was just going up to him to wish him good-day, when the dogs of the house set on to the dogs that had accompanied us across the island, and there was immediately a free fight, a dozen or more being engaged in the combat. I quickly jumped on to the top of a large wooden bowl that was lying in a corner of the house, but one of our party, not so fortunate, received a bite on the leg. With some difficulty peace was restored; and then, descending from my pedestal, I paid my respects to the king, who I found understood a few words of English. He appeared to me to be very ill, or else half drunk, I could not quite make out which. He asked me what I wanted, and I told him I wanted to anchor and to trade with them, but that I could not find anchorage; and I asked for a pilot to show me a passage through the reef, and requested him to send off one of his men for that purpose.

To my surprise, he immediately volunteered to come himself, and that if I would wait a few minutes, he would get ready to go off in my boat.

While he prepared to start, I walked down to the edge of the lagoon; but what a great sea it was!—the islands that I knew existed on the opposite side were too far off to be visible, and to right and left a chain of small, low islands stretched away till they sank below the horizon. Several fine canoes were lying on the beach, in every respect similar to the one that had come off to us at Bonham Islands. Whilst inspecting these canoes, I was summoned by the natives; and, on looking round, was surprised to see his majesty come out of the house carried on the back of a native, who immediately took the path across the island, in the direction of my boat. I thought this a somewhat extraordinary mode of proceeding, but made no remarks, supposing it was the custom of the country for majesty to be conveyed in this manner about the island.

When we reached the boat, the king was tumbled into it in what appeared to me rather an unceremonious manner,—and I began to think that he must really be intoxicated; however, he spoke quite sensibly, only making a slight objection when I refused to take three or four of his natives in my boat. I allowed him two companions, thinking this was quite enough, for my crew had a long pull before them, over a calm sea, under almost a vertical sun. He was so anxious to steer that I allowed him to take hold of the tiller, but in a very short time I found that he was nodding off to sleep. I woke him, and he remained awake for a short time, only to fall off to sleep again—in fact, he behaved as if he were in church. He objected to my relieving him of the duty of steering; but still, for the whole distance, which amounted to some six miles, I was employed in constantly nudging him to keep him awake.

On reaching the vessel, I jumped on board; and looking over the side of the schooner to see why the king did not follow, I saw him in the water, holding on to the side of the boat, his face streaming with blood. He was assisted up the ship's side by one of the natives, and sat down on deck. Seeing his face still bleeding, I fetched him some plaster and doctored him up generally, but still I confess I could neither make head nor tail of him; and I saw my sailing master smiling at the idea of my having brought off such a creature as a pilot.

I now went down below to have some luncheon, and on coming on deck, found our royal pilot asleep. Then I saw something that he had managed to conceal from me before. The soles of both feet were almost entirely gone, and where they ought to have been, I saw now a horrid raw cavity, which was sickening to look at. I awoke him, and invited him to have something to eat, and then asked him what was the matter with him, and hinted at the condition of his feet. He at once told me that some years ago he had undertaken a war expedition against the island of Majeru, where he had been wounded by a poisoned arrow; and although he had survived it, he had to a great extent lost the use of his limbs, and, in addition, was suffering from a number of horrible sores in different parts of his body. This appeared to me a sufficient explanation for his eccentric conduct, and I concluded that the poison had thoroughly got into his system.

After he had eaten, I questioned him about anchorage, and in which direction it lay. Of course for the present there was no prospect of moving, for the heaving sea was as polished as glass, and not a breath of air was stirring. He suggested our retracing our course, and anchoring at the north side of the group; but he also informed me that there was anchorage round the southern side.

We decided to adopt the latter, and when the

breeze sprang up towards night, we sailed slowly towards the south. At night it blew very hard from the east, and as, sailing south, we got beyond the shelter of the land, we found ourselves in a very heavy sea; we therefore went about to the north to get into smoother water and remain there till daylight. Next morning we found ourselves under the lee of two small islands, called Knox Islands on the chart, separated from the main group, but enclosed in a circling reef of their own. We were very much surprised at this, for by our chart, which was one of Imray's, 1872, Knox Islands ought to have been at least ten miles clear of the main group. As it was there was only about half a mile between them. It was blowing very hard right in our teeth, but we decided to attempt the passage. A very heavy swell rolled in against us, and the wind was so violent that we had to reef the sails. However we beat part of the way in; but I was fearful that in so heavy a sea, with light canvas, she would miss stays, and that we should be thrown on one or other of the savage reefs on either side of us, added to which the water was so shallow that the bottom was plainly visible, and all about I could see green patches of water, betraying still shallower places. However we made one or two boards, but finding we made but little progress, the vessel was put round, and we ran under the lee side of the island, determined to try and communicate with the natives somehow or other. The water was smooth and pleasant under the lee of the main islands, and in a short time we saw several large sailing canoes coming off, crowded with natives. Down they came to us, and, aided by the strong breeze, they literally seemed to fly over the smooth water. It was a wonderfully pretty sight, for each in succession rounded to under our stern, and then seeing we had some of their own countrymen on board, they sailed up to us, made their canoes fast to the vessel, and jumped on board.

In one of these canoes there was another king; and I find that the chiefs may always be distinguished from the common people by their being tattooed in parallel blue stripes from the base of the ear to the chin.

I bought everything they had got, and, at my request, some of the canoes went on shore again to fetch fowls, bread-fruit, and other island produce. As the breeze blew steady and strong we were enabled to stand in close with the land, which induced many smaller canoes to come off. In addition to island produce in the way of bread-fruit and cocoa-nuts, I succeeded in buying many mats, about three feet square, on which was woven in brown and black a very pretty pattern.

The men wore heavy grass girdles, similar to those I had seen at Baring's Island, under which they had bustles, which made their skirts stick out from their sides; these bustles were generally composed of cord, plaited over with fine straw, worked into a variety of patterns, and wound many times round their waists.

Straw hats were brought off in great quantities, and were eagerly purchased by my crew; the temptation was certainly great, for the price was only two small sticks of tobacco. Here too, as at the Kingsmill Islands, they make rolls of food prepared from the pandanus; this is tightly pressed, and carefully packed in many rolls of matting, and is said to keep for a very long time. In appearance it is like glue or toffee, and has a sweet taste, not pleasant to a European.

We appeared to have exhausted their supplies

about 3 in the afternoon, and therefore, landing our lame king and his suite, we stood away southwards. I was sorry not to be able to anchor at any of these places, but the weather was so uncertain, and the season was so far advanced, that I decided not to wait. Added to this, these low coral islands appear most uninteresting, and I had some similar ones to visit on my voyage to New Zealand.

The Russian captain Kotzebue claims the discovery of many of these islands in 1816, and appears to have been charmed by the inhabitants.

He says, but on what grounds I know not, that "it is certain that the Radack Chain has been peopled much later than most of the South Sea Islands; but whence and at what period is quite unknown. They have no tradition on the subject. Their language is quite different from all the Polynesian dialects, and appears of more recent formation. Whence have these people derived characters so much superior to those of other South Sea Islanders, many of whom, enjoying a fine climate and a more bountiful soil, resemble beasts of prey? I attribute this in some measure to the superior purity of manners among the females. . . . Upon perfect conviction I give a decided preference to these islanders over the inhabitants of Tahiti."

I may remark that the language of these islanders is very similar to that of the Kingsmill group, and that their high tone of morals must have undergone a considerable change since the time of Captain Kotzebue.

Soon after leaving this group we passed through vast fields of floating timbers, similar to those we had seen in the same latitude when sailing north for the island of Bonabi; and now as we neared the equator, and for some days after crossing it, we met with a current setting very strongly to the westward, which, with the light winds we experienced, fairly swept us out of our course.

CHAPTER VIII.

ON Thursday, Nov. 13th, at 6 A.M. we sighted Oitapu, one of the Ellice group. The island is purely of coral formation, low and sandy, but thickly covered with cocoa-nut trees; it unfortunately possesses no harbour. Oitapu is celebrated for its surgeons. Natives of other islands suffering from hydrocele come here to be cured. As far as I could learn they have some system of tapping their patients, which is usually successful. Not a few Rotumah chiefs have after a stay of a few months in Oitapu returned home perfectly cured.

We sailed close past the land, and at 11 A.M. came up with the island of Nukufatau. This island barely rises above the water, and cannot be seen at any great distance, the first thing to catch the eye being the tops of the cocoa-nut trees rising above the horizon.

Nukufatau is in the shape of a horse-shoe, and with its reefs encloses a lagoon about five miles in diameter. There is a passage through the reef and good anchorage inside. Three of my crew were natives of this place, and pointed out the passage at once. A stranger would hardly discover it, for the water in the passage is not very deep, and there is such a rush of tide running through it, that the sea breaks in the passage almost as much as it does on the coral reef on either side. We, however, stood boldly in, and the tide, which was now flowing, swept us in at a great rate, almost neutralizing the vessel's powers of steering. After passing through this break in the reef, we sailed on a mile or more over the smooth water of the lagoon, and then, as the bottom ahead of us looked rough and rocky, we dropped our anchor in ten fathoms, about three-quarters of a mile from the land.

Nukufatau may be taken as a specimen of a genuine coral island, and the nearer it is approached the more barren it looks. It consists of several long narrow strips of sand, scarcely rising above the sea, but here and there thickly covered with cocoa-nut trees. The island is never more than two or three hundred yards across, and in some places so narrow that one could jump over it. In addition to the two larger islands, which only differ from the smaller in their length, there are several small sandy islets situated on the reef that forms the lagoon. All the inhabitants are collected on one of the larger islands. Soon after we had cast anchor we were visited by several small canoes from the shore. The natives on recognizing their three fellow-countrymen on board, gave them a friendly but by no means demonstrative greeting, and after a few minutes' conversation took them on shore in their canoes. On enquiry I was disappointed to find that I could get little or no provisions at this island, which used to be famous for the number and excellence of its pigs. It is true the natives still had pigs, but they were few in number, and they did not care about selling them; so that it was only through the efforts of my three Nukufatau sailors that I managed to procure one or two. However, although fresh meat was scarce, we were always able whilst anchored here to get abundance of fish, for in addition to those we killed by explosions of dynamite, or caught with hook and line from the vessel's side, we purchased every morning from the natives several basketsful of flying fish. These they catch always at night. A perfect fleet of small canoes go out, each having a net set up on one side of it. The natives then light a flaming torch, towards which the fish fly, like moths to a candle, only to fall into the net set ready to receive them. The flying fish here attain the size of a herring, and though somewhat dry, like all ocean fish, they are by no means unpalatable, and we watched each morning with anxiety for the arrival of the fishermen's canoes. To secure the fish they always had to go outside the reef into the open sea, and each night their countless torches, rising and falling with the swell of the ocean, formed a very pretty spectacle. With the exception of these fish, and some cocoa-nuts, there was literally nothing to be bought from the natives. The soil of the island is so miserably poor, being entirely composed of sand and coral débris, that nothing but cocoa-nut palms and pandanus will grow, and on these the natives subsist.

I was very anxious to replenish our stock of fresh

water here, which was getting low, but we found that there was only one well on the island. This, too, was situated in the middle of an ancient burial-ground, and only about ten feet deep. The water, though perfectly fresh, rises and falls in the well with the tides of the sea; at high tide there are about eighteen inches of water in the well, at low tide little or none. However, a few casks were sent on shore, and with the assistance of the natives we managed to fill them, but it was a very laborious process, for the water had to be dipped out with cocoa-nut shells, which were emptied into a bucket, and this, when filled, was in its turn emptied into a cask.

It is indeed wonderful that this people, many of whom have visited better countries, should be found contented and willing to stay on such an island, when there are rich and fertile islands like Rotumah within a few days' sail of them. The abundance of cocoa-nuts makes up for the scarcity of water; their common drink is cocoa-nut milk, and I fancy that they seldom make any use of this well.

The natives are a remarkably fine-looking race, one of the finest in the Pacific; tall and well made, with features in many instances reminding one of the west of Ireland. They are certainly the fairest race we visited, and the women excel in good looks those of any of the other islands.

So fair are they that their cheeks betray a faint blush of pink. Amongst them there are a few Albinos, but they did not appear to be healthy; their hair is flaxen, their skin much freckled, and more the colour of a white pig than that of a European. Altogether, they have a decidedly raw and unhappy appearance. There is a native of Samoa living here as missionary, a graduate of the London Missionary Society's college in Samoa. He proved himself a most worthy fellow, and was very useful to our photographic party. In return for his kindness I made him some small presents. Next day I received a visit from two natives, who brought me a letter and a small parcel containing a pearl shell fish-hook and two old shell adzes; some of which latter I had been endeavouring to get from the natives, but without success, for they always answered my inquiries by assuring me that there were none now in existence. The letter, which was clearly and neatly written with pen and ink, ran thus :—

"Mr. Wood in the Vassl."
Mr. Wood these is boyes I have sent with yous Plece I love very much did you oblige me yesterday anythings from you I find it she look very niese. I am Sapolu

Nukefatau Nov 17 1873.

I never have quite made out what he wished me to understand, but I could gather from it that he appeared to be pleased with what I had given him. His wife also sent me off a boiled fish and three fans.

A man would certainly have to be to the manner born to be able to endure an existence spent on such an island as this. There would be very little amusement or occupation. The natives themselves have no employment whatever except fishing and picking cocoa-nuts; the women, it is true, work some coarse mats; but it would be madness to attempt to cultivate the soil. Still, with so much idle time, these people are happy; nor does the moral attached to Dr. Watts' "busy bee" seem to hold good here— Satan does *not* appear to "find some mischief still for idle hands to do." The whole population amounts to about two hundred.

Just imagine two hundred English men and women in a like position. What quarrelling, what scandal-mongering, what mischief-making would exist, so long as two families were left on the island, with plenty to eat and nothing to do!

I think it will be apparent to every one who visits these islands that the system adopted by the London Missionary Society of employing Samoan teachers, educated at the Society's college, is a most excellent one. The Samoan teacher is able to fill his position and perform his duties at far less cost to the society and with greater proportionate success than a white man.

Between a European and a coloured race there is ever a great gulf fixed. Your European missionary, be he never so condescending, be he never so gentle, loving, and earnest, cannot properly identify himself with his flock. He may gain the respect and even the dutiful love of the people amongst whom he lives, but from the entirely different construction of his mind, he can never thoroughly sympathize with them, or really understand their character, so strange a mixture is it of childish simplicity and impetuosity with low crafty cunning. The Polynesian teacher, on the contrary, stands on the same ground with his flock, he can understand the hopes and fears and aspirations which would occur to the native mind, and is able to discriminate between real or affected simplicity and cunning. From being of a similar nature, he is in every way able to enter into their feelings, and can lead and direct them as a pastor, without being obliged to rule them as a priestly potentate.

But besides all this a "native" missionary has this advantage, that he can live much as he would live in his own country, and sees his wife and children looking contented and happy, and therefore he can go about his work cheerfully.

The European missionary, on the contrary, has on many islands to endure the misery of seeing his wife pine away, and his children growing up without education, with evil surroundings and no constitution. And I maintain, that under such circumstances no man can do his work properly. He becomes miserable, gloomy, and jaundiced, his views of life and religion are coloured accordingly, and, perhaps unwittingly, he endeavours to make his native flock take a similar view of things.

Hence it is that laughter, song, and dance are everywhere suppressed, and the natives supposed to be on perpetual " Sunday behaviour." The melancholy consequence of this is, that the so-called Christian congregations grow up to be a set of hypocritical humbugs.

It would be a far pleasanter task to sit down and write a glowing account of the success of missions, and the wonderful spread of Christianity, but I cannot do it with truth. No one can deny that the missions have done much good, but I do not think that the result corresponds to the reports of the various societies or that the subscriptions are judiciously laid out. The Christian religion as introduced by our missionaries in the South Seas, appears to pass over a country like a tidal wave, that presently recedes and leaves it worse than ever, as witness the results in New Zealand and Fiji. And I think this in a great measure arises from a want of method. We take away from converted natives their dancing, their singing, and their manly sports, but nothing is given to supply their place. I believe that this dancing and singing and wrestling, &c. were natural and necessary habits of exercise to them, and that in taking these away we ought to have sent out missionaries to teach them some useful trade, such as carpentering, boat-building, &c., for without such habits of industry their moral condition can never be improved. Many intelligent Christian natives have told me that with the introduction of Christianity a kind of stupor has fallen on the people—they become idle and shiftless.

By the Wesleyan Missionary Society, which has so successfully extended its influence over the Fiji and Friendly Islands, large sums of money, and many tons of cocoa-nut oil, are collected from the natives annually. But it appears to me that, when so collected, it is a pity that it should be taken away from the island on which it is subscribed. For instance, in an island like Rotumah, I would expend it in making roads, and in the general improvement of the island, that is, in teaching the natives how to form cotton plantations, and how best to grow oranges and pine-apples, &c., for which they would always find a ready market in the Australasian colonies. All this kind of produce is at present quite neglected by the natives. I have only mentioned a few resources of these islands; but it is only by encouraging the natives to develope them, that we can make them a happy, healthy, and self-reliant people.

So long as we continue to imagine that the missionary should be a mild and reverend-looking person, standing under a palm-tree, addressing a crowd of natives who have collected to hear the glad tidings of the Gospel, and who are supposed to have nothing else to do from morning to night: so long as interesting little missionary reports are printed, which would lead one to suppose that these unfortunate natives were born for no other purpose but to supply the societies with easy and happy death-bed scenes: so long as deputations mount the Exeter Hall platform and, in the spirit of the chairman of a tottering insurance company, hold up to the meeting an unfair report of their position, there will never be any real success.

It is time to strip our missionary undertakings of this false atmosphere of romance, and look at them with plain common sense.

Our present system is to send out a missionary who teaches natives to read and write. This is excellent, but there we leave them, and are contented to see them sprawling about in their houses, smoking, eating, and sleeping, occasionally rising with a yawn to listen to a sermon or a prayer, and so they exist day by day, and as a consequence the race grows feeble and gradually disappears.

If they were taught that habits of industry were a necessary adjunct to the Christian religion, they would not so perish before our eyes.

It is written, " The Lord God took the man, and put him into the Garden of Eden *to dress it and to keep it.*"

The marvellously rich soil of these islands was never intended to be idle. If the present race are proved incapable of turning it to account, they will fade away before another and more energetic race, that must in course of time occupy the whole of these Pacific Islands.

On the 18th of November we sailed out of the lagoon, bound once more for Rotumah. On the 20th we sighted it and anchored at 4 P.M. off the village of Ouiaf. Here I remained two days, getting a plentiful supply of pigs and vegetables. These latter were a great treat, for we were weary of bread-fruit and taro, and had not been able to buy yams since leaving the Solomon Islands. Here I landed the Rotumah portion of my crew, who, by the way, wanted sadly to go on with me, and then I bade farewell to the South Sea Islands.

On the 27th, we passed the Island of Kendavu, and without further adventure sailed on, till at 10 P.M. on the 7th of December, we dropped anchor in Auckland Harbour.

THE END.

CHISWICK PRESS :—PRINTED BY WHITTINGHAM AND WILKINS, TOOKS COURT, CHANCERY LANE.

www.ingramcontent.com/pod-product-compliance
Lightning Source LLC
Chambersburg PA
CBHW021839230426
43669CB00008B/1020